PENGUIN PASSNOTES

Of Mice and Men and *The Pearl*

Marsaili Cameron was educated at the University of Aberdeen where she read English Literature and Greek. After a period of teaching in Scotland she entered publishing and now works in partnership with Gillian Hanscombe, producing books in a number of different fields.

PENGUIN PASSNOTES

JOHN STEINBECK

Of Mice and Men and *The Pearl*

MARSAILI CAMERON, M.A.
ADVISORY EDITOR: STEPHEN COOTE, M.A., PH.D.

PENGUIN BOOKS

PENGUIN BOOKS

Published by the Penguin Group
27 Wrights Lane, London W8 5TZ, England
Viking Penguin Inc., 40 West 23rd Street, New York, New York 10010, USA
Penguin Books Australia Ltd, Ringwood, Victoria, Australia
Penguin Books Canada Ltd, 2801 John Street, Markham, Ontario, Canada L3R 1B4
Penguin Books (NZ) Ltd, 182–190 Wairau Road, Auckland 10, New Zealand

Penguin Books Ltd, Registered Offices: Harmondsworth, Middlesex, England

First published 1986
Reprinted 1988

Interactive approach developed by Susan Quilliam

Made and printed in Great Britain by
Richard Clay Ltd, Bungay, Suffolk
Filmset in Monophoto Ehrhardt

Contents

To the Student   6
Background to John Steinbeck   7

Summary: *Of Mice and Men*   13
Commentary: *Of Mice and Men*   19
Characters: *Of Mice and Men*   40
Themes: *Of Mice and Men*   46
Glossary: *Of Mice and Men*   51

Summary: *The Pearl*   55
Commentary: *The Pearl*   62
Characters: *The Pearl*   81
Themes: *The Pearl*   84
Glossary: *The Pearl*   88

Passages for Comparison   91
Discussion Topics   94

To the Student

The purpose of this book is to help you appreciate John Steinbeck's novels, *Of Mice and Men* and *The Pearl*. It will help you to understand details of their plots. It will also help you to think about the characters, about what the writer is trying to say in each novel and how he says it. These things are most important. After all, understanding and responding to plots, characters and ideas are what make books come alive for us.

You will find this Passnote most useful after you have read the text you are studying through at least once. A first reading of the novels will reveal their plots and make you think about the lives of the people they describe and your feelings for them. Now your job will be to make those first impressions clear. You will need to read the novels again and ask yourself some questions. What does the writer really mean? What do I think about this incident or that one? How does the writer make such or such a character come alive?

This Passnote has been designed to help you do this. It offers you background information. It also asks many questions. You may like to write answers to some of these. Others you can answer in your head. The questions are meant to make you think, feel and respond. As you answer them, you will gain a clearer knowledge of the novels and of your own ideas about them. When your thoughts are indeed clear, then you will be able to write confidently because you will have made yourself an alert and responsive reader.

Note: Double quotation marks are used in this Passnote for words and phrases taken directly from John Steinbeck's work.
The page references are to the edition published by Pan Books. This Passnote is published with the permission of William Heinemann and Pan Books.

Background to John Steinbeck

Born in the small town of Salinas, California, in 1902, John Steinbeck was the son of a schoolteacher and a mill manager. His grandparents on both sides of the family were immigrant settlers. The family was not well off, and the young John Steinbeck took a number of part-time jobs to earn money. He also spent as much time as he could exploring the California countryside in search of wildlife. This countryside provides the setting for many of his novels, including *Of Mice and Men*.

He started writing short stories while still at high school; but his academic career at Stanford University was a patchy one. He dropped out of college for two years and made a living from a variety of jobs, including field work on a ranch. This experience he put to good use when writing *Of Mice and Men* fifteen years later. Steinbeck returned to university but left without a degree. He had already started work, however, on *Cup of Gold*, a novel about Morgan the pirate which was to be his first published work.

In the next few years, Steinbeck found – and lost – several jobs, including those of reporter and caretaker. In 1930 he married Carol Henning, who helped to support him while he wrote. Publication of *Cup of Gold* in 1929 was followed by *The Pastures of Heaven* (1932), *To a God Unknown* (1933) and *Tortilla Flat* (1935); this last work became a best-seller and gave Steinbeck some financial independence.

In 1936 he started work on what was to become *Of Mice and Men*, a short novel set among migrant farm workers. This work was, he wrote in a letter, "a tricky little thing designed to teach me to write for the theatre". Originally entitled 'Something That Happened', Steinbeck intended the novel to be "a study of the dreams and pleasures of everyone".

The book had an unfortunate start in life. "Minor tragedy stalked," wrote Steinbeck in a letter. "I don't know whether I told you. My setter pup, left alone one night, made confetti of about half my manuscript book. Two months of work to do over again. It sets me back. There was no other draft. I was pretty mad but the poor little fellow may have been acting critically. I didn't want to ruin a good dog for a manuscript I'm not sure is good at all. He only got an ordinary spanking with his punishment fly swatter. But there's the work to do over from the start."

When the book was published in 1937, it was re-titled *Of Mice and Men.* Taken from the poem 'To a Mouse', by the eighteenth-century Scottish poet, Robert Burns, the title carries echoes of this other writer who was deeply involved in the lives of men working on the land. The phrase is found in the following lines from Burns' poem:

> But, Mousie, thou art no thy lane
> In proving foresight may be vain:
> The best-laid schemes o' mice and men
> Gang aft a-gley,
> And lea'e us nought but grief and pain
> For promised joy.
>
> Still thou art blest, compared wi' me!
> The present only toucheth thee:
> But och! I backward cast my e'e
> On prospects drear!
> And forward, though I canna see
> I guess and fear.

The book was instantly successful in terms of sales; and Steinbeck soon began work on a stage version. His collaborator, George Kaufman, an eminent director and writer of the time, commented that, 'It drops almost naturally into play form and absolutely nobody knows that better than you.' The play proved a considerable success on Broadway in New York and won the esteemed Drama Critics' Circle Award. In 1939 a film of the book was released.

Familiar with migrant working conditions since his time at high school and Stanford, Steinbeck expressed his anger and compassion in articles for newspapers and magazines. These feelings are also to be found in passionate form in novels such as *In Dubious Battle* (1936) and in what many consider his greatest work, *The Grapes of Wrath* (1939).

An important friendship in Steinbeck's life was with Ed Ricketts, a scientist based in Monterey. Sharing an intense interest in the biology of sea creatures, the two men joined in a scientific expedition into the Gulf of California (off the coast of Mexico) to study and collect marine life of the shoreline. The log of their journey was published in 1941 as *Sea of Cortez*. The idea for *The Pearl* had come to Steinbeck during their sea voyage; and, in fact, *Sea of Cortez* had already referred to the story of a young Mexican and a great pearl. *The Pearl* itself, the story of a Mexican fisherman's finding and losing of a treasure, was published in 1947.

Too old for military service when America entered the war, Steinbeck wrote a book on the US Air Force to help boost recruitment; he also spent six months at the front as a correspondent for the *New York Herald Tribune*.

Steinbeck's first marriage broke down in 1942, and in 1943 he married a dancer, Gwen Verdon. The couple settled in New York and had two sons, but this marriage also ended in divorce. In 1950 Steinbeck married Elaine Scott.

Steinbeck's later work included screenplays, travel writing and more novels, including *East of Eden* (1952), a story which became familiar to many through the film starring James Dean. Steinbeck travelled a good deal, both in America and in Europe. In the 1950s and 1960s he became more politically active, writing condemnations of the Communist-hunting Senator Joseph McCarthy and campaigning vigorously on behalf of Lyndon Johnson, who became President after the assassination of John F. Kennedy. The 1960s also brought many literary awards, including the Nobel prize in 1962.

John Steinbeck died in 1968, after a series of illnesses.

Of Mice and Men

Summary: Of Mice and Men

Scene 1: pp. 7–20

John Steinbeck introduces us first of all to a place: a clearing on a wooded riverbank where a path ends up at a deep, green pool (p. 7). In the evening of a hot day, two men appear in the clearing (p. 8). When Lennie drinks thirstily from the pool, George warns him sharply that the water may not be fresh. They sit by the pool (p. 9).

Complaining about Lennie's bad memory, George reminds him that an employment agency has sent them into the country to work (p. 10). Lennie has been playing with a dead mouse and George takes this away from him. George also tells him not to open his mouth in front of the boss at the ranch where they are to work (p. 11).

Lennie is sent to get wood for a fire (p. 12) but comes back holding only one small stick. Realizing that Lennie has gone in search of the mouse, George makes him give it up, and throws it far away (p. 13). George reminds Lennie how, when he had mice as pets, he used to kill them by accident (p. 14).

After Lennie has fetched more wood, George lights a fire and starts to heat some cans of beans. Lennie says that he likes beans with ketchup and George loses his temper (p. 15). He accuses Lennie of being a burden on him and always getting him into trouble, like when people thought Lennie had attacked a girl (p. 16). Lennie offers to go away, alone, to the hills; but George tells him that he wants him to stay.

Lennie then asks George to tell him "about the rabbits" (p. 17). Telling what is clearly a familiar story, George describes to Lennie how one day, unlike other ranch hands, the two of them will have a little place of their own (p. 18). While they have supper, George tells Lennie to come back to the clearing if he gets into trouble again (p. 19). They lie down to sleep (p. 20).

Scene 2: pp. 20–37

It is ten in the morning (p. 20), and an old man is showing George and Lennie which bunks to take at the ranch's sleeping quarters. George complains that the bunk-house isn't clean but the old man denies it (p. 21). He also tells them that the boss is angry because they didn't turn up for work that morning (p. 22).

When the boss comes into the bunk-house, he complains to George and Lennie about their lateness; George offers an excuse for this (p. 23). The boss becomes suspicious of the fact that George is doing most of the talking (p. 24); and, after warning George not to be "a wise guy", the boss leaves (p. 25). While George is telling Lennie off for opening his mouth in front of the boss (p. 25), he discovers the old man outside the door. The old man denies the charge of eavesdropping.

A young man, Curley, comes into the room looking for the boss, his father (p. 26). Catching sight of Lennie, he becomes aggressive and tries to make him talk (p. 27). After Curley leaves, the old man tells George that Curley is an experienced boxer (p. 27); but George replies that Lennie could make short work of him (p. 28). According to the old man, Curley's recent marriage has made him even more aggressive. His wife, apparently, still has an eye for other men (p. 29). When the old man has gone, George tells Lennie to try to avoid Curley (p. 30); but, if he gets into any kind of trouble, to go back to the clearing by the river (p. 31).

Curley's wife appears in the bunk-house, saying that she's looking for Curley. Lennie thinks that she's pretty but George doesn't like the way she talks to them (p. 32). After she has gone, George gives Lennie a fierce warning to stay away from her.

Slim, the leader of one of the work teams, comes into the bunk-house and speaks in a friendly way to George and Lennie (p. 34). When another man, Carlson, joins them, it comes out in conversation that Slim's bitch has just had puppies (p. 35). Curley suggests that the old man, Candy, should shoot his dog and take one of Slim's puppies. When Carlson and Slim leave the room, Lennie and George discuss the possibility of Lennie's getting one of the puppies too (p. 36). Curley comes in looking for his wife and exchanges a few unfriendly words with George; George and Lennie then leave to find their dinner (p. 37).

Scene 3: pp. 37–61

It is evening in the bunk-house and George and Slim sit down to talk (p. 37). George thanks Slim for giving a puppy to Lennie; he is then drawn into talking about how he and Lennie have ended up travelling together (p. 38). He and Lennie, he says, have got used to each other (p. 39) – although Lennie does often get into trouble, like on the recent occasion when a girl mistakenly accused him of attacking her (p. 40). Lennie comes in and goes straight to his bunk, hiding the puppy that he is carrying. Undeceived, George sends him away to take the puppy back to its mother (p. 41).

When Candy and Carlson come in from playing horseshoes, Carlson starts complaining about the smell from Candy's old dog (p. 42). Carlson claims that it would be kinder to the dog to shoot it now rather than let it linger on. But Candy is reluctant to take this decision. Slim agrees with Carlson (p. 43).

The discussion is interrupted by the entrance of another ranch hand, Whit, who is anxious to show Slim a magazine (p. 44). Refusing to be distracted, Carlson presses Candy to agree to the shooting of the dog; he produces his Luger pistol in readiness. When Slim says nothing, Candy agrees, miserably (p. 45).

After Carlson has taken the dog, several attempts to engage Candy in conversation fail; George and Whit sit down together at the card table (p. 46). Eventually, the sound of a shot is heard (p. 47).

Crooks, the black ranch hand in charge of the stable, appears, and asks Slim to go with him to the barn. While playing cards, Whit and George talk about Curley's wife (p. 49). They agree that her presence seems likely to cause trouble on the ranch; Whit then asks George to join himself and the others the following night on a visit to the local brothel (p. 49). A few minutes after Carlson and Lennie return to the bunk-house, Curley bursts in, asking if anyone has seen his wife or Slim (p. 50). When he hears that Slim is in the barn, he dashes out, closely followed by Whit and Carlson (p. 51).

Lennie tells George that Slim has told him not to pet the pups so much; he also says that Curley's wife hasn't been in the barn. George expresses his worry about the set-up on the ranch (p. 52) and goes on to describe in detail the place which he and Lennie hope to get someday (p. 53). Lennie asks George to tell him exactly how he, Lennie, will care for the rabbits they will keep (p. 54). When Candy joins in the conversation, George is suspicious at first but listens quietly to Candy's proposal that he should contribute his savings and join in the scheme (p. 55). After doing some calculations, George realizes that their dream may now be within their grasp (p. 56). Greatly excited, the three decide to leave the ranch after a month; but George cautions them against telling anyone of their plans. Candy adds sadly that he should have shot his dog himself (p. 57).

Slim returns to the bunk-house, accompanied by Curley, Carlson and Whit. When Slim warns Curley to leave him alone, Curley looks around for someone to vent his rage on. He picks on Lennie (p. 58). Lennie is reluctant to fight back but, urged on by George, he seizes Curley's fist and crushes it; the fight is finished (p. 59). Before Curley is taken away to a doctor, Slim makes him promise not to tell anyone that it was Lennie who hurt his hand (p. 60). George reassures Lennie that he is not in trouble this time (p. 61).

Scene 4: pp. 61–75

Crooks, the "stable buck", has his living and sleeping quarters in the harness room (p. 61). Lennie comes to this room on Saturday night and, unsuccessfully at first, tries to make friends with Crooks (p. 62). After Lennie has explained that the others have gone into town and that he, Lennie, has been looking at the pups in the stable, Crooks softens a little and tells Lennie to sit down (p. 63).

In conversation, Lennie lets slip the secret of the planned-for land (p. 64); Crooks reacts by mocking Lennie's friendship with George (p. 65). When Crooks mentions the possibility of George's not coming back, Lennie advances threateningly on him; but is slightly placated by Crooks's explanation that loneliness lies behind his mockery (p. 66). Crooks reminisces affectionately about his childhood on his father's ranch, but casts scorn on Lennie and George's dream of land of their own (p. 67).

Candy joins the two men in Crooks's room (p. 68) and the talk turns again to the dream of land. Fiercely, Candy defends their plans against

Crooks's mockery (p. 69). Impressed despite himself, Crooks offers to come and help.

On the appearance of Curley's wife, the men fall silent and sullen – apart from Lennie who is fascinated (p. 70). When Curley's wife tries to find out what happened to Curley's hand, Candy tells her that he got it caught in a machine; a lie which she rejects angrily (p. 71). Stung by the insults which she has directed at them, Candy tells her that they have land of their own. Unconvinced, she notices the bruises on Lennie's face and works out that it was he who hurt Curley (p. 72).

Candy tells her to leave Lennie alone; and Crooks demands that she leave his room. Curley's wife turns viciously on Crooks, threatening him with terrible punishment (p. 73). Telling her that he has heard the men coming back, Candy urges her to go away; but, after she has gone, Crooks has lost all heart for the project (p. 74). George appears and scolds Lennie and Candy for talking about their plans (p. 75).

Scene 5: pp. 75–88

It is Sunday afternoon and all the ranch hands except Lennie are playing horseshoes outside. Lennie is sitting in the barn looking sorrowfully at the puppy, which he has just killed by accident (p. 76). Worried that George will punish him, he debates what to do until, suddenly, Curley's wife appears beside him and tries to draw him into conversation (p. 77).

Although Lennie attempts to avoid talking to her, Curley's wife wins him over by sympathizing about the puppy's death (p. 78). Going on to talk about her earlier life, she expresses resentment over lost hopes and opportunities (p. 79). The conversation turns to Lennie's dream farm and rabbits; Lennie explains that he likes rabbits because they are soft to touch (p. 80). Curley's wife then invites him to feel her hair but, when his hand is heavy on her head, she gets angry and screams (p. 81). In a panic, Lennie tries to silence her but, when she continues to scream, he shakes her angrily. This breaks her neck (p. 82).

Frightened at what he has done, Lennie remembers what George said about going back to the clearing and he leaves the barn (p. 82). Curley's wife lies undisturbed, peaceful in death, until Candy comes into the barn; on discovering the dead body, he leaves again, quickly (p. 83).

Candy returns to the barn with George, who immediately realizes how Curley's wife has met her death; the two men discuss what is to be done (p. 84). George decides that the other men must be told what has happened; but he asks Candy to give him a few minutes' start before the news is broken (p. 85). After expressing his rage and disappointment over his lost dreams, Candy fetches the other men. Curley immediately identifies Lennie as the killer and goes off to get his shotgun (p. 86). He returns to the barn with Carlson, who says that his Luger has been stolen; assuming that Lennie has taken it, Curley expresses his intention of shooting Lennie on sight (p. 87). George is forced to join the hunting party; while Candy is told to stay with the dead woman (p. 88).

Scene 6: pp. 88–95

It is late afternoon in the clearing by the river and Lennie comes out of the brushwood to drink from the pool (p. 88). Sitting by the river, he wonders to himself how George will treat him now; in his imagination his Aunt Clara scolds him for being a burden on George (p. 89). An imaginary giant rabbit then appears to him (p. 90) and threatens that this time George will leave him.

When George himself comes to the pool, he calms Lennie down and they sit silently while the shouts of the searching men come from a distance (p. 91). Puzzled that George doesn't seem angry with him, Lennie encourages him to tell the familiar stories about the two of them, together and alone (p. 92). George asks Lennie to turn his head and look across the river while he, George, tells him how things will be; meanwhile, unseen, George takes Carlson's Luger out of his pocket (p. 93).

The distant voices come nearer and, after reassuring Lennie that he isn't angry with him, George shoots him in the back of the head (p. 94). The other men from the ranch burst into the clearing; George pretends that he has taken Carlson's gun away from Lennie in a struggle. Understanding something of what George is going through, Slim leads him gently away (p. 95).

Commentary: Of Mice and Men

Scene 1: pp. 7–20

Do you know where Soledad is? Or the Salinas river? Judging by the first sentence of *Of Mice and Men*, John Steinbeck seems to think that you, the reader, probably do know where these places are. In fact, they are in California, in the United States of America, some way south of San Francisco.

Perhaps you feel that it doesn't matter where the story is set? Well, you'll find as you study the book that John Steinbeck is a writer who is very keen to help you really join him in his story. He wants you to hear, see, smell – and sometimes taste and touch – the life that he's introducing you to.

Take another look at the scene described on pp. 7 and 8 before the arrival of George and Lennie. There is a lot of life there by the pool, although most of it isn't human life; jot down some of the sights and sounds found there.

When George and Lennie appear, walking towards the pool, you'll see that John Steinbeck introduces them very carefully. Even before they speak a word, we know quite a lot about them. Look at the following pieces of information given to us and note down what they tell us about the two men.

1. Both wear denim clothing.
2. Both carry blanket rolls.
3. One man lags behind the other, even in the open clearing.
4. One man is neat, quick and restless.
5. The other man is big and cumbersome, moving like a bear.

By the time you've done this, you'll probably have realized just how much you already know or can guess. The two men are the same in some ways, aren't they, and different in others? Have you noted, for example, that the kind of clothes they're wearing probably show that they are working men – and that the blanket rolls they both carry indicate that they are used to being on the move? As for the differences between the men – well, it's quite clear already, isn't it, that one is the leader and the other the follower?

This initial impression is deepened once the men start exchanging words with each other. Would you think it was fair to say that George treats Lennie rather like a child? What words and actions of George's would prompt you to say this? And does Lennie in fact speak and behave like a child? In what ways does he do this?

After they've both drunk some water and sat down by the pool, George starts complaining about having been forced to walk so far in the heat. When Lennie shows that he has forgotten where they're going, George snaps at him and calls him "a crazy bastard". Look again at this section and at the following conversation on p. 10. Do you think that George is really angry with Lennie at this point? What evidence would you give to back up your opinion?

You may well have decided that George isn't really angry with Lennie; that he uses terms like "crazy bastard" in an affectionate rather than insulting way. Do you ever pretend to be angry or grumpy when you don't really feel that way at all? Or do other people ever pretend to be angry with you? In what sort of relationship would either of these things happen?

If you agree that George isn't really angry here, what does this tell us about George's relationship with Lennie? Jot down your thoughts on this, adding them to the conclusions you came to earlier about whether George treated Lennie like a child. As we read on, you'll find that you'll need to think a good deal about the relationship between the two men. Keep notes on your thoughts as you go along.

When reading the conversation on p. 10, you may have got the feeling that you were eavesdropping; that is, listening in on a conversation not primarily meant for your ears. There's the mysterious mention of "the rabbits", for example, and the unexplained reference to "Murray and Ready's". You'll probably get this feeling again several times as you read on: John Steinbeck has written his book almost like a play, so that much of the information we need comes to us through conversation among the characters. What we must do as readers is listen carefully, remember as much as we can, even if we don't understand it immediately ("the rabbits", for example) and, when we're given enough hints, guess (like, for example, guessing from what else George says that Murray and Ready's is an employment agency).

The episode when George discovers that Lennie has a dead mouse and takes it from him tells us a great deal more about the two men. George clearly knows Lennie very well indeed; and Lennie clearly has some rather odd tastes – like petting dead mice. What else does this episode tell us about George and Lennie?

On pp. 11–12 George gives Lennie instructions on how he is to behave at the ranch where they are to work. We learn at least two things from this: one, how bad Lennie's mental concentration is and, two, the fact that Lennie got into trouble at the last place where they worked. Do you think that George is patient or impatient with Lennie at this point? Why do you think this?

George has decided that he and Lennie should spend the night in the clearing. Read again, on pp. 13–14, the description of how Lennie retrieves his mouse and is then found out by George. Imagine that you're Lennie and write down a brief note on how you felt during this episode. Then imagine you're George and briefly describe the different emotions you felt.

Look again at the part of the conversation (on p. 14) where George and Lennie discuss what happened to the live mice Lennie used to keep as pets. How does this point forward to the climax of the book?

Together, George and Lennie prepare and light a fire so that they can heat up their supper. Have you ever built – or helped to build – a campfire or bonfire? Does the passage on p. 15 remind you of that experience? In what ways was your bonfire different?

George loses his temper when Lennie says, for the second time, that he likes beans with ketchup. Is George really angry this time? What makes you think this? Even if you do decide that he is really angry, do you think that he means everything he is saying? When you lose your temper, do you sometimes say things you don't really mean? Try to remember the different things George says to Lennie: we'll come across them again much later in the book.

Lennie is frightened by George's outburst; but the two men make friends again quite quickly afterwards. Note that George does not apologize. How then do they manage to smooth over the harsh words?

This time, try to remember what Lennie says to George: again, we'll come across his words much later in the book.

At last (p. 12), we learn what Lennie has meant by talking about "the rabbits". He and George have a story they tell each other (although George does most of the talking). The story is about how loneliness and despair can be driven away by friendship. George and Lennie reassure each other that, unlike other ranch hands, they have a future ahead of them. Protected and encouraged by each other, they will someday get a little place of their own where they will grow crops and keep animals (including rabbits). (Did you recognize the phrase "Live off the fatta the lan'" on p. 18? Try it with an American accent ... Written 'properly', it would read "Live off the fat of the land" – a phrase which comes from the Bible and means 'live well and have the best of everything'.) Do you feel sympathetic towards George and Lennie's dream? Why do you think they have this dream? Do you think either of them believes that it will become reality some day? Do you ever have dreams of this kind? How would your dream be different from the one described here?

While they have supper, George tells Lennie to come back to the clearing if he gets into any kind of trouble. He also warns him that if he does get into trouble, he won't be allowed to tend the rabbits. Do you feel that the author is preparing you, the reader, for future happenings? How do you feel about the thought of Lennie getting into trouble?

Scene 2: pp. 20–37

We're told quite a lot about the inside of the bunk-house, the big room where the ranch hands sleep. When they're not sleeping, how do the men spend their time there? Would you like living in a bunk-house, do you think? What would you like or dislike about it?

The old man cleaning out the bunk-house is anxious to reassure George that the place is clean. Notice what he says about the previous occupant of George's bunk: that he "used to wash his hands even *after* he ate"? Did you find that a funny remark? As well as being quite amusing, this episode tells us about the fairly rough conditions that the ranch hands have to live in. What does it also tell us about the kind of man George is?

The boss is angry, the old man says, because George and Lennie didn't arrive in time to go out to work that morning; and as usual, the boss took his anger out on the "stable buck". (He's the hand who stays at the ranch and looks after the livestock and tackle.) The old man explains this by saying that the stable buck is a "nigger". Remember that this story was first published in America in 1937. How do you think most white people regarded black people at this time? Read again the section of dialogue from the middle of p. 22 to the top of p. 23. The boss clearly feels that the colour of the stable buck's skin provides a good enough reason for treating him badly; but do you think that the old man and the other ranch hands share his attitude?

When he does appear, the boss doesn't waste many words, immediately asking George and Lennie to account for themselves. Do you get the impression that George is used to dealing with awkward questions from bosses? What might give you this impression?

Look towards the bottom of p. 23, at the sentence beginning, "George scowled meaningfully at Lennie . . ." What is it that Lennie has understood? If you're not sure, look back to the middle of p. 11.

The boss is suspicious of the fact that George is doing most of the talking, answering for Lennie as well as for himself. Why is the boss suspicious? What does he think Lennie is up to? What might this tell us about the boss himself? George tells the boss that Lennie is his cousin; do you think he is telling the truth here? What might suggest that he's making this up?

After the boss has gone, George turns sharply on Lennie. He is angry because he's afraid. What is George afraid of? Do you ever get angry with other people when, really, you're afraid for yourself or for them?

George thinks that the old man has been listening in on their conversation. Do you think that George is right in this – or do you believe what the old man says? (A "swamper" is an odd job man.) Why is it that George doesn't "like nobody to get nosey"? And what does the old man mean when he says "a guy on a ranch don't never listen nor he don't ast no questions" (p. 26)? Do you agree with the old man that the boss is "a nice fella"? And what do you think he means by "you got to take him right"? Jot down three words which you might use to describe the boss.

The conversation between Curley and George is even more difficult and uneasy than the previous conversation with his father, the boss. Look back to that earlier conversation (pp. 23–25) and then make a note of the similarities and differences between the two conversations.

Now look back at the notes you've made. Have you included as a similarity the point that both Curley and his father are in a position of power over George and Lennie? And have you noted as a difference the fact that Curley seems to be on the brink of threatening physical violence?

Notice, towards the bottom of p. 27, what George says about Curley: "Say, what the hell's he got on his shoulder?" Did you catch the reference? George is referring to the phrase 'a chip on his shoulder', meaning something like 'a grudge against the world'. George is wanting to know what's wrong with Curley, that he's so needlessly aggressive.

The old man is happy to talk about Curley. As we saw earlier, much of the information we need as readers is given to us through conversation between the characters. Read again the section from the bottom of p. 27 (sentence beginning, "The old man looked . . .") to two-thirds of the way down p. 29 (sentence ending, "There's plenty done that . . ."). The following pieces of information are contained there; put them in the order in which we learn them.

1. The old man is frightened of Curley.
2. Curley has become even more aggressive since his recent marriage.
3. Lennie doesn't like fighting.
4. Curley's wife is pretty and hasn't let marriage dampen her interest in other men.
5. Curley is a good and experienced boxer.
6. Whatever he does, Curley won't get sacked, being the boss's son.
7. George has no doubt that if Curley and Lennie start fighting, Lennie will win.
8. Lennie doesn't know any boxing rules.
9. Curley is a small man who hates bigger men.

You'll probably have noticed that, although we've only met one of the new characters involved (Curley), we now have a pretty clear picture of how things are at the ranch – and how they might develop.

Once George and Lennie are left alone, George warns Lennie about the possible dangers ahead. How does Lennie react to George's warning? Do you think that George is giving Lennie the right advice? Why do you think this? Have you worked out what "get the can" and "plug himself up for a fighter" (both on p. 20) probably mean? The first means 'get the sack' and the second means 'get well known as a fighter'.

As the conversation develops between the two men, we see again how dependent Lennie is on George. Note down two examples of this from p. 31. What is your first impression of Curley's wife? Do you think that this is the impression that the author wanted to get across? What makes you think this? Now re-read p. 32 and the first half of p. 33 and think about how she appears to Lennie and to George. Jot down some notes on the differences in their reaction to her; then use these notes to write a paragraph describing the differences.

After she has gone away, Lennie suddenly expresses the wish to leave the ranch at once; but George tells him they must stay. Do you feel that George is making the right decision at this point?

Read through the description of Slim on p. 34. Jot down five words that tell you what Slim is like. Some phrases may have puzzled you in the description. A "jerkline skinner" is a mule driver who controls several animals with one rein. A "bull whip" is a long, plaited rawhide whip with a knotted end. A "wheeler" is the wheel horse – that is, the horse that follows the leader and is harnessed next to the front wheels. "Butt" you probably know: it means the hindquarters. And what about the point about his hands being like those of a temple dancer? Well, in traditional dancing in certain countries in Asia the hands are the focus of attention, being used with great skill and grace.

Slim's friendly first words to Lennie and George may also contain some unfamiliar words and phrases. "It's brighter'n a bitch outside", for example, means that the sun's light is very strong; and "punks" don't here go in for safety pins or spikey hair; they're just inexperienced young men.

After Carlson joins in the conversation, we learn two things that are to become important: one is that Slim's bitch has just had puppies; the second is that Carlson wants the old man, Candy, to shoot his old dog. Did you guess, like George did, that Lennie was bound to want one of the puppies?

Curley makes another brief and angry entrance – to be greeted very coldly by George. Do you think George should have behaved any differently at this point?

Scene 3: pp. 37–61

Their day's work over, George and Slim are talking in the bunk-house. Lennie has been given one of Slim's puppies, it seems; and he has also proved his strength during the afternoon's work.

Like the boss earlier in the day (p. 24), Slim comments on the fact that George and Lennie are so friendly. (You may have noticed, on p. 35, that Slim had already mentioned this.) How do you think Slim's attitude to their friendship differs from that of the boss? Notice how what Slim has to say about the life of most ranch hands echoes what George said much earlier to Lennie (pp. 17–18).

It is during this conversation between George and Slim that we find out how George and Lennie first got friendly with one another. (Can you remember the lie about this that George told the boss? If not, look back at p. 25.) George says that at first he used to play tricks on Lennie. What made him stop doing this?

Slim comments that a "guy don't need no sense to be a nice fella . . . Take a real smart guy and he ain't hardly ever a nice fella". Is this true, do you think? Can you think of people you know who would fit these descriptions?

During this same conversation, we also find out exactly what kind of trouble Lennie got into at the place where they used to work. This is a list of some of the things that happened; put them in the correct order.

1. George and Lennie hide in an irrigation ditch.
2. George hits Lennie over the head with a fence post.
3. Girl screams more loudly.
4. Lennie reaches out to feel the dress.
5. George and Lennie leave the area at night.
6. Lennie sees a girl in a red dress.
7. A lynch party is organized to go after Lennie.
8. Lennie gets confused and holds on tight to the dress.
9. George hears the screams and comes running.

10. Girl lets out a scream.
11. Girl tells the police that she has been raped.

Imagine that you're the girl in the red dress, and write down what you felt happened when Lennie touched your dress. Then imagine that you're Lennie, and describe these same few minutes after you touched the girl's dress. Which set of feelings do you find it easier to describe? Why?

By this time in the story, you should have a pretty good idea of what Lennie and George are like as people. Write down some words that you think describe them and then write a paragraph about each of them (you'll probably find it helpful to use the notes on their relationship that you started keeping when looking at Scene 1).

Lennie comes into the bunk-house, hiding the puppy under his jacket. You'll probably agree with Slim (p. 42) that this time George does treat him just like a child. Jot down notes on how exactly he does this.

After Candy and Carlson come into the bunk-house, the conversation turns again to what should be done about Candy's old dog. Why is the old man reluctant to shoot his dog? Do you think that you would feel the same in his position? If you've read the whole book already, you'll realize that this exchange between Candy and Carlson sheds some light on future events in the lives of Lennie and George. Make notes on how it does this.

Why do you think the author introduces an interruption here in the shape of Whit's excitement over the magazine? Would you agree that at least two purposes are served by it? One is that the episode shows us that Carlson is determined not to be diverted from his goal of having the dog put down. The other is that we learn something more about what kind of people the ranch hands are and what kind of dreams and ambitions they have. Remember what we've already been told about Western magazines on p. 20? Jot down some thoughts on what kind of people you think they are (do they find their own lives exciting and fulfilling, for example?).

As we have seen, Slim's opinion is law in the bunk-house; and Slim has indicated that Carlson is right to shoot the dog. Candy can do nothing more to save him. Imagine that you're Candy after the dog has been taken away. Remembering all the things that we've been told about Candy and the dog (like, for example, that he's had him from the time he was a puppy), write an account of the main feelings that sweep over you as Candy.

While Candy lies silent on his bunk, the other men try to start up a normal conversation. You'll probably agree that they're not very successful in doing this. Why does their attempt not work?

After the shot has been heard, the atmosphere in the bunk-house becomes a bit more relaxed. While George and Whit play cards, Slim follows Crooks out to the barn. What news has Crooks brought about Lennie? From everything you've heard so far, how would you describe Lennie's approach to the puppies?

When Whit goes on to talk about Curley's wife, he echoes much of what Candy told George earlier. How would you summarize this? George too echoes his own earlier words when he says, "She's gonna make a mess." Do you agree that by this time we, as readers, have a strong feeling that trouble of some kind is brewing?

Like all the ranch hands, Whit uses a lot of slang, some of which may be unfamiliar to you. Let's look more closely at the passage where he describes to George "the usual thing" done by the ranch hands on Saturday nights (p. 49). The "place" he's talking about is a brothel. If you don't know the meaning of that word, look it up in a dictionary. What word would you use? When George asks him how much it costs, he answers "two an' a half", meaning two and a half dollars. By a "short" he means a drink, a measure of spirits (probably whisky); and by "two bits" he means a quarter (25 cents). "A flop" refers to a sexual encounter with one of the women in the brothel.

Whit goes on to tell George that there are two rival brothels in town: Susy's place and Clara's. Susy's place is more fun, says Whit, and it's cheaper too. Susy thinks that Clara is stuck-up for no good reason (a "kewpie doll lamp" means a lamp that looks like a certain kind of doll — small, fat-cheeked and wide-eyed, with a curl of hair on top of the head). Indeed, Susy is in the habit of hinting to her customers not only that Clara overcharges (that's the meaning of "getting burned" at the top of p. 50) but that the women there may pass on some nasty diseases (that's the meaning of the following sentence, beginning "There's guys around here..."). "A crack" has the same meaning as "a flop"; and "goo-goos" means foreigners of one kind or another.

Lennie and Carlson come into the bunk-house. While Carlson is cleaning his Luger pistol (remember that he has this gun – it becomes important later), he tells the others that Curley, as usual, is looking for his wife. When Curley himself comes in on this quest, he also asks for Slim and, on hearing that he is in the barn, leaves in angry haste. What does Curley suspect? Whit and Carlson follow him to see what happens. What do they hope to see?

Meanwhile George finds out from Lennie that although Slim is in the barn (he has told Lennie not to pet the pups too much), Curley's wife has not been there. How would you describe George's attitude to this whole situation? George then goes on to give his opinion that on the whole the safest place for women is in a brothel; outside it, if they're young and attractive (he uses the words "jail bait" (p. 52) and "tart" (p. 53)), they usually cause trouble for men.

If you're a girl, you may be feeling a little besieged, attacked or left out by this point in the story. After all, nearly all the likeable or admirable characters so far have been men; the women in the story may seem to you either not very important or not very nice. Take a minute, if you're a girl, to note down your feelings about this aspect of the story; if you're a boy, make notes on what you imagine you might feel if you were a girl.

Lennie is more interested in rabbits than in women. When he asks George about the place they hope to buy some day, old Candy turns over on his bunk to listen. Why do you think that this conversation might attract his interest when the earlier ones didn't? Remember the earlier notes you made on the dreams of the ranch hands.

Re-read the section from p. 53 to the top of p. 55 where George describes their dream ranch. First, make notes on where and how they hope to live; then write two paragraphs describing their life there. Would you like to live like that? What would you like about it?

When Candy first speaks, Lennie and George are startled and seem to feel guilty. George also becomes suspicious. Why might they react in this way? Candy then goes on to offer his savings (why does he have so much saved?) as contribution to the project if only George and Lennie will let him join them in this scheme. Re-read p. 56, then make notes on why Candy is so anxious to join in (". . . they'll put me on the county" is the equivalent of 'I'll have nowhere to live and only Supplementary Benefit to live on').

How do George and Lennie react when they realize that their dream could become a reality? Do they react differently? If so, how? George is anxious that no one else should know about their plans. (Did you get the meaning of the sentence on p. 57 beginning, "They li'ble to can us . . ."? It means, 'They're likely to get us sacked so that we can't save up the money we need.') Why do you think George might feel this way?

Notice what Candy says to George about feeling that he should have shot his dog himself. Why do you think he feels this? Think of the end of the story if you've read that far; why is it significant that he makes this remark to George in particular?

When Slim, Whit, Carlson and Curley come back to the bunk-house there's a lot of bad feeling in the air. Curley starts half-apologizing to Slim for his suspicions; but, when he's taunted by Carlson and Candy, he gets ready to lose his temper again. Why does he pick on Lennie in the end? And how does Lennie react? Do you remember why Lennie reacts in this way? (If not, look back to p. 31.)

Re-read the description of the fight on pp. 58 and 59, making notes on what happens. Then write an account of the fight from Lennie's point of view. Remember to include all the main things that happened and how you, as Lennie, felt at these different points.

Once the fight is over, Lennie backs against the wall. He has won the fight; but does he feel triumphant and pleased with himself? Have you ever felt similar things to Lennie after you've won a fight?

Slim makes arrangements for Curley to be taken to a doctor; but, before he is taken away, Slim makes Curley promise not to tell his father that it was Lennie who hurt his hand. How does Slim manage to get Curley to promise this?

Did you notice that George says something particularly important when he's explaining why Lennie did so much damage to Curley's hand? Slim (p. 60) has assumed that Lennie was very angry; but George says, no, it wasn't anger Lennie felt – it was fear. Remember that much the same thing happened in the struggle with the girl in Weed? Lennie, it seems, is at his most dangerous when he's afraid.

Do you believe Lennie when he says that he "didn't mean no harm"? Why have you made this decision? What is Lennie most afraid of happening as a result of the fight?

Scene 4: pp. 61–75

Crooks, the ranch hand based in the barn (the "stable buck"), lives in a little one-room lean-to beside the barn itself. The description of his room (p. 61) tells us quite a lot about his interests and how he spends his time. Note down a list of some of the objects in the room, along with ideas on what these objects tell us about Crooks.

Crooks is at home, alone, on Saturday evening, rubbing ointment into his twisted back. (Do you remember how he damaged his back? If not, look back to p. 22.) When Lennie appears in the doorway, Crooks angrily tells him to go away. What are the reasons Crooks gives Lennie for this unfriendly reception? Do you think that if you were in Crooks's place, you would react in the same way?

Lennie tells him that the other ranch hands, including George, have gone into town for the evening. What reasons does Lennie give for coming to the barn? Is Crooks satisfied with these reasons? Why does Crooks ask Lennie into his room in the end?

From the start of the conversation, Crooks makes it clear that he doesn't believe in any of Lennie's schemes or plans. He seems much more interested in finding out more about the friendship that exists between Lennie and George. Do you get the feeling at this point (p. 64) that Crooks is behaving a bit like an interrogator who asks questions not out of friendly interest but for some other, perhaps sinister, purpose?

As he talks on, we begin to get some idea of what this purpose might be. Crooks, it appears, has always led a pretty isolated life: in his youth he was the only black child among many white children and now, as an adult, he is the only black hand on the ranch. During his life he has learned to mistrust white people (see the sentence on p. 64, "But I know now") and therefore avoid them as much as possible. But he has not been able to escape the miseries of loneliness. And so, when he sees a close friendship between two other people, he is overcome with envy and finds the sight of such friendship difficult to bear.

Would you agree that it's probably for this reason that Crooks torments Lennie with suggestions that he may be abandoned by George? How does Lennie react to Crooks's "supposin'" about George? Why does he react in this way, do you think?

Once Lennie is no longer threatening violence, Crooks goes on to explain that he only wanted Lennie to get an idea of the loneliness felt by him, Crooks. Crooks then describes just how he feels during his long evenings alone. Have you ever experienced anything like the feelings he describes? If you're black, describe any occasion when you too felt excluded from some activity or group " 'cause you was black" (p. 66). If you're white, describe any occasion when it occurred to you to wonder if someone was being excluded from an activity or group because of the colour of their skin.

Lennie is barely half-listening to what Crooks is saying; but as soon as Crooks starts describing his peaceful childhood home, Lennie's interest is attracted. Would you agree that both have dream ranches in their minds – but Crooks's dream is in the past and Lennie's is in the future? Crooks goes on to explain why he is so impatient with Lennie's plans for the future. What are the reasons he gives?

When Candy appears, looking for Lennie, Crooks greets him in an abrupt and unfriendly way, just as he at first greeted Lennie. We learn, however, that really Crooks is delighted to have visitors. It turns out that, although Candy and Crooks have worked on the same ranch for years, this is the first time that Candy has been in Crooks's room. How does Candy react to the invitation to come into the room? ("I do' know" means 'I don't know': the apostrophe shows that a letter has been dropped.) And how does Crooks respond to Candy's embarrassment? (Explain the humour in Crooks's remark beginning, "Sure, . . . and a manure pile . . .")

Crooks resumes his attack on their plans. What sort of thing does he say to try to discourage Lennie and Candy? Why do you think he is attacking them in this way? Does he succeed in discouraging them? Read Candy's speech at the bottom of p. 69 and make notes on why Candy is so determined that their dreams will come true.

Crooks is clearly taken aback to hear that nearly all the money needed to buy the place is already saved. Always in the past, it seems, men who seem to be desperate for their own land have in fact wasted their money in brothels and gambling dens. What offer does Crooks go on to make to Lennie and Candy?

When Curley's wife appears, it soon becomes clear that she's not really looking for her husband; she knows very well that Curley has gone to town with the rest of the men. How does she explain the fact that the ranch hands – apart from Lennie – don't like to be seen talking to her? Look on p. 71 at what Curley's wife has to say about her life; then, imagining that you're her, write notes, then a paragraph, about what it's like being married to Curley. Do you feel sorry for her or not? Why do you feel this way?

Curley's wife doesn't hesitate to insult the three men in front of her. How do the men react to these insults? Make sure that you describe the differences in their reactions. What gives Candy the courage to talk back to the boss's daughter-in-law? Do you think he's ever done such a thing before? Although Curley's wife scornfully rejects what he has to say, you may feel that at the end of the conversation it is Candy who emerges with dignity. Why might you feel this?

Curley's wife has already made it clear that she doesn't believe the story that Curley's hand was caught in a machine. Seeing the bruises on Lennie's face she now guesses correctly that he was the "machine" in question. Is she angry with Lennie for hurting her husband? If not, how does she seem to feel towards him?

When Crooks too finds the courage to ask her to leave them alone, Curley's wife turns on him with a viciousness we haven't seen before. Did you catch what she meant when she asked, "You know what I could do?" She meant that simply by claiming that Crooks, a black man, had tried to assault her, she could send him to a hideous death by lynching (that is, illegal hanging). Such murders by white lynch mobs were by no means uncommon in the USA at that time.

How do Crooks, Candy and Lennie react to this threat? After Curley's wife has gone, the atmosphere has changed in Crooks's room. How would you describe the change? How do you account for it? Are you surprised when, after George has collected Lennie and Candy, Crooks calls out to Candy to forget about his previous offer to work with them on the ranch? Why does he do this?

Scene 5: pp. 75–88

When we first enter the barn on Sunday afternoon, it seems a very pleasant place to be. It's full of hay, the horses are making contented noises; from outside we can hear the sounds of men happily playing horseshoes. But then we see something that gives us a shock. What do we see?

Lennie is clearly upset that the puppy is dead. But he feels a number of other emotions as well. Here's a list of some of the things he feels; put them in the order in which he expresses them.

1. A faint hope that George won't be angry with him.
2. Regret and sorrow that he hadn't paid more attention to the advice given him about the puppy by George and Slim.
3. Fear that, if he finds out what has happened, George won't let him look after the rabbits.
4. Realization that George will know that he, Lennie, is responsible for the puppy's death.
5. Grief over his growing conviction that the death of the puppy means that he'll never be allowed to look after the rabbits.
6. Anger with the puppy for letting itself be killed.
7. Belief that he can pretend to George that he, Lennie, had nothing to do with the puppy's death.

Unnoticed by Lennie, Curley's wife comes into the barn. How does Lennie react when he first sees her? Although she seems keen to talk to him, he is determined not to be drawn into conversation with her. What reasons does he give for this? How does she try to persuade him that it's all right for him to talk to her? (A "tenement" is a 'tournament', a series of games at the end of which a winner is declared.)

Curley's wife is rather taken aback when she discovers what Lennie is hiding. Write a paragraph explaining how the puppy died. How does she try to cheer up Lennie?

When Lennie is still unwilling to talk to her, Curley's wife gets angry. Re-read, on pp. 79–80, what she says about herself and her life. First make notes on what we learn about her earlier life; then write a paragraph describing the main events. Do you believe that the man in "pitchers" ('pictures', 'films') really did think she was a "natural" as an actress?

Why else might he have said this? Do you think that her mother (her "ol' lady") really did steal the letter? If not, what do you think happened?

Do you feel any differently towards Curley's wife now that you know more about her? What words would you use to describe her? Does her eagerness to speak about herself without interruption remind you of anyone else in the story – of Crooks, for example, in the previous scene?

Lennie has claimed that he is listening to her; do you think that he really is? What do you think is actually going on in Lennie's mind? When the conversation turns from rabbits to the other kinds of things Lennie likes to pet, you may feel that danger is brewing. In his excitement, Lennie has clearly quite forgotten George's strict instructions not to talk to Curley's wife. How does Curley's wife react to Lennie's dropping his guard against her? What do you think she wants from Lennie?

Re-read the account of what happens from when Lennie first strokes the woman's hair up to the time when he realizes that she is dead (that is, the middle of p. 82). First make notes on the different things that happen; then write a paragraph describing exactly what happens.

How did you feel when you read the account first of all? Although shocking, the sequence of events may have seemed quite familiar to you. You were remembering, perhaps, what we were told earlier about several other events: the 'attack' on the girl in Weed, for example; the death of Lennie's pet mice when he was a boy; the wounding of Curley; and, most recently, the death of the puppy. Note down the most important things that all these events have in common.

What are Lennie's reactions once he realizes that Curley's wife is dead? Are these the reactions that you would expect from him? Why?

After Lennie has gone to hide in the brush, the barn becomes peaceful once again. Even Curley's wife is peaceful in death. What is the first thing that old Candy thinks when he comes into the barn and sees Curley's wife?

George too thinks at first that Curley's wife is asleep; but, as soon as he realizes that she is dead, he also realizes how she met her death. Why do you think George says, on p. 84, "I should of knew . . ."? What does George think should be done about Lennie? Why does he think this? And how does Candy respond to this suggestion? How do you think George feels when Candy mentions the likelihood of a lynching?

The worst moment for Candy comes when George confirms by his silence that the dream ranch will now never be bought. Candy is haunted by the thought of the happy life that will now never happen; George, on the other hand, has his eyes only too clearly fixed on the reality of the life that awaits him. What kind of life is that likely to be?

George says that "Lennie never done it in meanness..." What do you think he means by the word "meanness"? Do you agree with this judgement of Lennie?

After George and Candy have made arrangements to 'cover' George from suspicion of being involved in the killing, Candy pours out his anger and sorrow in a speech to the dead woman. Write a paragraph describing the different emotions he expresses. Do you think that he's fair to the dead woman? If she were alive, how do you think that she might answer old Candy?

Candy then leaves to fetch the other ranch hands. Re-read the description (p. 86) of Curley's first reaction to the sight of his wife's dead body. How would you describe this reaction? Is it the reaction you would expect from a husband who really cared for his wife?

George and Slim discuss the different options open to them for dealing with the problem of Lennie. Note down the different alternatives, along with the arguments for and against them.

When Carlson appears, shouting that Lennie has stolen his Luger pistol, you may suspect that he has picked on the wrong man. Who do you think has taken the gun? Why do you think this?

The search party sets out, armed with a shotgun at least, leaving Candy behind with the dead body. Why do you think "Curley's face reddened" (p. 87) when he refused to stay with the body? Watching the face of the dead woman, Candy murmurs "poor bastard". Who is he thinking of, do you think, as he utters these words? Why do you think this?

Scene 6: pp. 88–95

As the end of the story approaches, you'll see that we've come full circle as far as the setting is concerned. Back at the deep green pool by the Salinas river, we are once again looking at how nature occupies itself when there are no human beings present.

When Lennie appears, he comes "as silently as a creeping bear moves"; and the impression we have of him drinking from the pool is almost that of a weary animal. Do you think this is a suitable image for Lennie? Why?

Lennie is talking to himself – perhaps to reassure himself and to make himself feel less alone and frightened. He expresses several different feelings about his situation; note down the different feelings as he expresses them.

After this, rather an extraordinary thing happens. Lennie's imagination gives birth to a human figure, a little old woman, who proceeds to scold him. And this figure, we soon find out, is Lennie's Aunt Clara (we already know that she is now dead but that she looked after Lennie when he was young).

Why might Lennie be visited by a vision of Aunt Clara at this particular time? Would you agree that it might be partly because he's alone (we've already seen that Lennie doesn't like being alone; remember his evening visit to Crooks?) and partly because he feels that he has let George down particularly badly?

Write an account of the conversation between Lennie and the imaginary Aunt Clara. When you've done this, give a few moments' thought to two things. One is that it's most unlikely that the real Aunt Clara would use such powerful swear words! Such details make it clear to us that Lennie has indeed 'made her up' and is actually scolding himself. The other point is to do with what "Aunt Clara" says in the paragraph (p. 90) beginning, "All the time he coulda . . ." Look back to the top of p. 85 where George gives his own description of how his life will be without Lennie; how do these two accounts compare? Would you agree that it's clear that, although George used to be fond of telling Lennie how pleasant his life would be without him, he didn't really mean it at all?

The appearance of the imaginary giant rabbit marks the rise of further strong feelings of guilt and fear within Lennie. Note down the fears that the rabbit forces Lennie to confront.

George then comes out of the undergrowth and calms Lennie down. The first few moments of their conversation are rather different from usual – and clearly very different to what Lennie is expecting. What differences would you pick out as important? Have you included the fact that this time it is George rather than Lennie who is distracted and doesn't have much to say? As you read this section, did you pick up the reference to the "sound of men shouting to one another"? Who are these shouts coming from and what is the significance of them?

Lennie is relieved that George isn't going to leave him, but he's clearly puzzled that George doesn't seem to want to "give him hell". Why is it, do you think, that George has no inclination to get angry with Lennie? In the end, George is persuaded to say the things he usually says when he's in a rage with Lennie; but he speaks with difficulty and without feeling. Note down some examples of this.

Lennie then persuades George to speak about his favourite subject: the way in which he and George are different from the other ranch hands. (Remember when this was first mentioned, with the two of them sitting in the same place as they are now? Look back to pp. 17–18 if you've forgotten that conversation.) Again, George is having difficulty in getting his words out. Why is this? How does George's shaky way of speaking make you feel?

What prompts George to tell Lennie to take off his hat? What is in George's mind, do you think? We now learn for sure that it was George – not Lennie – who took Carlson's Luger. As Lennie looks towards the mountains, George is intending to shoot him in the back of the head. Why has George decided to do this? Do you remember what old Candy said to George (p. 57) about wishing that he had shot his dog himself? How do you think this may have affected George? Do you think that George has made the right decision? Why?

For the last time, George and Lennie tell each other the story of their dream ranch. Can you explain why many people find this passage very moving? Look at the dialogue from the top of p. 94 down to the point where George finishes speaking. You'll see that there's a double meaning in nearly everything that George says. George seems to be talking about the same things as Lennie, but he's also preparing himself for something that Lennie doesn't know is about to happen: that is, Lennie's own death. Make notes on the double meanings involved.

Like Candy's old dog, Lennie doesn't "feel a thing" when he is shot. But George clearly does. What mixture of emotions do you imagine George feels? How would you feel in his place?

Slim is the only one of the ranch hands to show any sign of understanding what George must be going through. How does he try to comfort him? The last word is left to Carlson, the man who insisted earlier on shooting Candy's dog. Why do you think that this rather insensitive character is allowed to end the story in the way he does?

Characters: Of Mice and Men

GEORGE

Because George, like Lennie, is one of the two central characters, it's not possible to get a full view of what kind of person he is just by reading a few selected sections of the book. We can get to know George only by paying careful attention throughout the story both to how we see him behave and to what is said about him, by himself and others.

The first time we meet George is on the Thursday evening in the clearing by the deep green pool. He's trying to persuade Lennie not to drink too much water: he knows that the water may not be fresh, but Lennie clearly doesn't understand that it may make him sick. You may well feel that this episode tells us a great deal about the kind of person George is, especially when he is with Lennie. Perhaps you would find it helpful to start off by writing down some words to describe how George comes across to us in this early part of the story. Would you agree that the words 'sensible', 'anxious', 'protective' and 'patient' are appropriate ones here? Now add your own suggestions to the list. Do you think that you could cope with Lennie as well as George seems to here?

Do you remember what Slim says about the friendship between George and Lennie? "It jus' seems kinda funny a cuckoo like him and a smart little guy like you travellin' together" (p. 38). It's certainly true, isn't it, that George does seem to be "a smart little guy"? After all, it's George who got them the jobs at the ranch; it's George who coped with the ugly situation in Weed when the girl was almost badly hurt by Lennie; it's George who can deal with bosses and difficult workmates.

If you re-read the section on pp. 39–41, you'll see that Slim was indeed right to call George "a smart little guy". However, you'll probably also find another way of seeing George reflected in these pages;

you may recognize a feeling that we've come across before in the story and a feeling that will be expressed very powerfully during later events. How would you describe this feeling? Would you agree that it's something like *need* on George's part? Although George likes to pretend sometimes that Lennie is nothing but a nuisance to him (see pp. 15–16, for example), the truth is that he needs Lennie just as much as Lennie needs him. In what ways do you think George does need Lennie? Give some examples from different parts of the story. One example might be that through the continuing story of the dream ranch, George and Lennie help each other to escape from the harsh reality of the life led by most ranch hands. What are the aspects of this life that George is most eager to escape?

Think about George's decision at the end of the book to shoot Lennie. What feelings do you think lay behind this decision? Write a paragraph to explain how shooting his friend could possibly be understood as a final proof of friendship on George's part.

Imagine that you can go forward in time ten years from the end of the story. Write a paragraph on how you think George is living then. Has he settled down in a place of his own, or is he still moving from ranch to ranch? Is he lonely or does he have at least one good friend? Does he still have dreams about the future?

LENNIE

Think about some of the destructive things that we see Lennie doing – or hear about him doing – during the course of the story. He used to crush pet mice to death, for example; when in Weed he hurt – or at least badly frightened – a young woman; he kills his puppy by accident; and, in the end, he breaks a young woman's neck. How does knowing about these things make you feel about Lennie? Do you think of him as a frightening, cruel person? If not, how would you explain why you *don't* feel these things?

Perhaps your answer to that question echoes what George says about Lennie on p. 85: "All the time he done bad things but he never done one of 'em mean." Lennie never *intends* to hurt anyone or anything; his problem is that he easily gets into a panic and when he's in this state he completely forgets that his great strength makes him very dangerous. Do you remember something else that George says about Lennie? On p. 42 he says, "There ain't no more harm in him than a kid . . . , except he's so strong." Note down some of the ways in which you think Lennie thinks and behaves like a child.

Did you include the fact that Lennie is very open and friendly to the people he meets? Like a child, he expects people to like him and to be nice to him. Think, for example, of his Saturday evening visit to Crooks when he is puzzled and dismayed by Crooks's unfriendly reception. What effect does this friendly approach have on other people? Would you agree that most people (including Crooks in the end) respond warmly to Lennie's affectionate nature and in turn show the best sides of their own natures? Try to think of some examples of this happening.

One obvious example can be found in the passage on p. 39, where George describes to Slim how Lennie jumped into the Sacramento River just because George told him to; and how Lennie's lack of resentment towards George made George ashamed of the way he had treated Lennie. It's clear that Lennie is almost totally dependent on George just as he was on his Aunt Clara. If George were not there to look after him, then Lennie would indeed probably end up in a "booby hatch", as Crooks suggests (p. 66). Would you agree that nowadays Lennie would be regarded as being 'mentally retarded'? Do you know any people who could be described in this way? How do you think about them and feel towards them? Does getting to know the character of Lennie make any difference to your attitudes?

CURLEY

We learn about Curley at six main points in the book: pp. 26–30, pp. 36–7, pp. 50–51, pp. 57–60, p. 71 and pp. 86–8. Look through these sections again carefully before you read on.

You'll probably have noticed that our first impressions of Curley are very much coloured both by George's reactions to him and by what Candy has to say about him. Do you think that George and Candy are good judges of character? Do you feel inclined to trust their judgement of Curley? Note down the main things that we learn about Curley from George and Candy.

You probably feel that George and Candy are proved right by later events. Curley does indeed continue to behave like a man who has a grudge against the world; he quite unfairly picks on Lennie for a fight, thinking that Lennie is too timid a character to fight back; and his lack of grief at his wife's death shows clearly that he saw her as a prize to fight over rather than a human being to love.

Can you imagine what it feels like to be Curley? Why do you think that he might behave in the way he does? Does Curley remind you of anyone you know? How do you feel about this person?

CURLEY'S WIFE

We learn about Curley's wife at five main points in the book: pp. 28–9, 31–3, 48–9, 70–72 and 77–82. Look through these sections again carefully before you read on.

As with the character of Curley, you'll have noticed that the information we're given about Curley's wife is heavily coloured by the views of the different men who describe her. What is the view taken of her by the three characters who have most to say about her – Candy, Whit and George? Why is it, do you think, that these three men hold very similar views? Do you feel that, as seems to be the case with Curley, there really is little that can be said about her except that she's a trouble-maker? While thinking about that, remember that she is the only woman among several men, most of them unmarried; it may strike you that any woman, whatever her personality, might find it difficult to feel at ease in this situation. Remember too that George has a special reason (his knowledge of what happened in Weed) to be afraid of the presence of a woman in a place where Lennie lives and works.

Curley's wife, you'll have noticed, is not even given a name of her own; she is known to us only by association with a man whom she doesn't even like (p. 79). From what she tells Lennie about her life and from the way that we see her behave, would you describe her as a happy or an unhappy person? If you've decided that you would describe her as an unhappy person, go on to give some examples of how her unhappiness causes her to behave in ways that upset other people.

Do you know anyone who reminds you of Curley's wife in any way? Have you ever thought that this person might be unhappy?

CROOKS

We learn about Crooks, the stable buck, at three main points of the book: p. 22, pp. 47–8, and pp. 61–75. Look through these sections again carefully before you read on.

You'll probably agree that the first things we're told about Crooks are very important for understanding his character. Do you remember the main things that Candy tells George about Crooks? He says that because Crooks is black, he gets the brunt of the boss's bad temper; he also tells George that Crooks suffers from a twisted back as a result of being kicked by a horse. If these were the only facts that you knew about Crooks, what kind of person might you expect him to be? Might you expect him to be open and friendly, for example?

During the course of the Saturday evening in Crooks's room (pp. 61–75), we discover a great deal about the stable buck's life, past and present. We soon learn, for example, that he is far from being open and friendly in his approach to people; but we also learn that, like Curley's wife, he is an unhappy and lonely person. Give some examples of how Crooks's unhappiness and loneliness cause him to behave in ways that upset other people.

Just as Curley's wife is the only woman on the ranch, so Crooks is the only black person; both suffer from a sense of isolation from other people. However, where Curley's wife has power – being white and also the daughter-in-law of the boss – Crooks can do very little to gain people's respect. Think for a moment about what happens when Crooks does stand up for himself and his new friends (p. 73). Imagining that you are Crooks, write a paragraph explaining how you feel after Curley's wife has made her terrible threat.

CANDY

We learn about Candy at six main points in the book: pp. 20–23, 26–30, 42–7, 53–8, 68–75 and 83–8. Look through these sections again carefully before you read on.

Like Crooks, Candy suffers from an injury at work: he lost his right hand in an accident. This means that, being crippled as well as old, he expects the boss to get rid of him quite soon. If this happens, he will have no home and only a little money saved up. How do you think John Steinbeck would like us to feel about this situation? Why do you think this?

Candy clearly keeps his eyes and ears open about the ranch: he knows a lot about what's going on, and he's quite willing to talk about what he knows to someone, like George, whom he considers to be a safe listener. However, Candy is usually careful to keep a low profile, avoiding any trouble or rows. Why is this, do you think? Would you agree that it's because, like Crooks, Candy feels that he is always in a weak position? Give some examples of occasions when Candy tries to remain unnoticed or otherwise shows that he feels powerless.

One of your examples may have involved Candy's attempt to shield his dog from Carlson's attention; and, on his failure to do this, his silent retreat to his bunk. What does Candy's dog mean to him, do you think? You'll probably agree that the dog is his best and oldest friend. Have you also considered the fact that Candy sees the way his dog is treated as a sign of the way he himself is regarded by others – for example, as old, worn-out, worthless?

Candy responds immediately and passionately to the dream which is so important to Lennie and George. Note down the different reasons why you think the dream ranch gripped his imagination so powerfully. What do you think will happen to Candy after his hopes are so cruelly dashed?

Themes: Of Mice and Men

FRIENDSHIP VERSUS LONELINESS

Think for a moment about the main characters in *Of Mice and Men*: George, Lennie, Candy, Crooks, Curley and Curley's wife. Which characters would you describe as lonely people? After answering that question, you may be surprised at the number of characters whom you do think of as lonely; and you'll probably have noticed that even if some of the characters are not lonely while the action of the story takes place, they were either very lonely in the past or they will be lonely in the future.

Would you agree that part of the message of the story is that people can still feel lonely even if they're surrounded by other people for much of the time? Think of Curley's wife, for example; although she has a husband, she can still say, "Think I don't like to talk to somebody ever' once in a while?" (pp. 71–2). Or think of Candy, an old man who lives with other people but whose best friend is a dog. Have you ever felt lonely even though you were surrounded by people – at school, for example, or at a party? Write a paragraph describing the occasion and how you felt.

Let's turn now to thinking about how loneliness can affect people. We hear about this a great deal during the story – and we see some of the effects of loneliness actually taking place. Do you remember what George says about ranch hands? Re-read the passage on p. 17 that starts, "Guys like us, that work on ranches, are the loneliest guys in the world . . ." Re-read too the passage at the bottom of p. 39, starting with the words, "I ain't got no people . . ." George is giving his opinion here that lonely men easily become aggressive and difficult characters. Can you think of examples of this happening in the book?

Crooks too describes vividly the effects of loneliness: "I tell ya," he cried, "I tell ya a guy gets too lonely an' he gets sick" (p. 66). Re-read what Crooks has to say about loneliness on pp. 66 and 67. Would you agree that part of what he's describing is how loneliness has indeed made him "sick"? Do you think that Curley's wife could also be described as "sick" from the same cause? Write a paragraph explaining what you would mean by this. In real life, have you ever met people whom you think might be "sick" from loneliness?

Something else that the book tells us about loneliness is how people can be so desperate for a listener that they hardly notice whether or not the other person is really interested in what they have to say. Can you think of any examples of this happening in the story? Several one-sided conversations may have come to your mind in thinking about this. There is that last, fateful, conversation between Lennie and Curley's wife, for example (pp. 77–81), where both people are too preoccupied with their own thoughts and worries to pay much attention to what the other person is trying to communicate. Or there is the earlier conversation between Lennie and Crooks (pp. 62–8) where Crooks not only takes advantage of Lennie's presence to talk about his life but also acknowledges exactly what it is that he is doing. Do you remember what Crooks says about this? "I seen it over an' over an' over – a guy talkin' to another guy and it don't make no difference if he don't hear or understand. Thing is, they're talkin', or they're settin' still not talkin'. It don't make no difference, no difference" (p. 65).

What do you feel about what Crooks says here? Have you ever felt glad of another person's presence even if you knew they didn't really understand your state of mind at the time?

Having looked at some of the effects of loneliness on people, let's think now about what the book tells us about the difference friendship and kindness can make to people's lives. Take Candy and Crooks, for example. Think for a moment about what sort of people they seemed to be when we first got to know them; then write a paragraph describing how they changed when they felt that other people had begun to take an interest in them.

You'll probably have noted down something like that both men showed a renewed interest in life and a new self-confidence. Where previously they had been locked up inside themselves with their worries and suspicions, once they were shown friendship they began to open out to the opportunities that the world might still offer them.

The most important friendship in the book, of course, is that between Lennie and George. In different ways, each helped the other to cope with life. Would you agree that John Steinbeck's account of this friendship, along with the others described in the book, conveys a message that nearly all human beings have a deep need for affection and respect? Do you agree with this view?

DREAMS VERSUS REALITY

Day-dreaming is important to most of the characters in *Of Mice and Men*. Lennie and George share a day-dream – about a small ranch that they will own one day – and the sharing makes the dream particularly powerful. As they discuss how they will live in the future, they encourage each other to heap up the detail, the place of their dreams all the time becoming more and more vivid in their minds.

Other characters have no one willing to share their dreams – but they continue to dream all the same. Think of Curley's wife, for example: she's constantly looking for opportunities to show the people around her that she's ill-suited to the restricted and boring life that she leads. In her head, she's a gifted actress who could have had a fabulously successful career in films. Or think of Crooks: his dreams focus on the past rather than the future, a past where he was surrounded by friends and relations and didn't know the meaning of loneliness. Even Curley – whom you may feel is the book's most unattractive character – can be seen to have his dream: that of being the 'hard man' of the ranch, feared and respected by everyone.

The dream cherished by George and Lennie is one, we learn, shared by a good many ranch hands. Do you remember what Crooks says about this? He tells Lennie: "I see hunderds of men come by on the road an' on the ranches with their bindles on their back an' that same damn thing in their heads. Hunderds of them. They come, an' they quit an' go on; an' every damn one of 'em's got a little piece of land in his head" (p. 67). What is it about this particular dream, do you think, that is so attractive to these men? After answering this question, take a minute to think about your own friends or fellow students. Is there a dream that you all have in common? What is this dream and why is it so important to you all?

In *Of Mice and Men*, the day-dreams remain just that – day-dreams: none of them are transformed into reality. Just like all the other ranch hands, George, Lennie and Candy are doomed never to set foot on their own piece of land. Curley's wife will never be an actress. Curley will continue to attract scorn rather than respect. And Crooks is almost certain to end his days a lonely man. Whenever dreams are put to the test in this book, they evaporate, disappear. Think, for example, of the scene in Crooks's room where Curley's wife viciously crushes the growing confidence of Crooks and Candy; or think how George and Lennie's dream begins to approach reality – only to be destroyed entirely.

Despite this, however, you may feel that the author is not suggesting that it's a waste of time to dream. Note down some of the positive aspects of day-dreaming shown in the story. You may want to include, for example, the fact that day-dreaming prevents some of the characters from falling into despair. Do any of the positive aspects you have noted down apply to day-dreaming in your own life? In what way?

INJUSTICE

In discussing the theme of 'injustice', we come to some of the reasons why the characters in *Of Mice and Men* find day-dreams so important in their lives.

Think of everything we're told about the lives of the ranch hands, for example. They are rootless men without a permanent home; they move from ranch to ranch, living with strangers on other people's property – and even eating food cooked always by other people. There's much hard work but little pleasure in their lives – so, when they save up a little money, the great temptation is always to spend it quickly in bar rooms and brothels. It's hardly surprising then that many of them dream of owning a little piece of land of their own.

Do you remember what Candy says about his working life? "I planted crops for damn near ever'body in this state, but they wasn't my crops, and when I harvested 'em, it wasn't none of my harvest" (p. 69). And do you remember too the situation Candy is in as he approaches an old age when he can no longer work? He has lost a hand in an accident at work and has been given a little compensation; but he knows that he'll soon be forced to leave the ranch and, as he says, "I won't have no place to go, an' I can't get no more jobs."

What do you think is the message that John Steinbeck is trying to convey through his descriptions of Candy and the other ranch hands? Would you agree that one of the things he is suggesting is that people who work hard and long deserve better than a life spent entirely at other people's service and an old age of poverty and despair? What are your own views on this subject? Why do you feel this way?

Let's look at another example of injustice to be found in the story. Crooks is black – and is clearly discriminated against because of his colour.

The boss takes out his rages on him; the other ranch hands pick on him, excluding him from card games in the bunk-house, for example. Curley's wife makes a dreadful threat against him: she threatens to accuse him of assaulting her and thus ensure that he will be lynched. Crooks knows well that the fact that the accusation is completely false would in no way save him from this dreadful fate. Black men and their families at that time had no reason to expect justice from their white compatriots; such threats therefore were a recurring nightmare for them.

Do you think that John Steinbeck thinks it right that black people should be discriminated against because of their colour? You'll probably agree that the way in which the character of Crooks is presented suggests strongly that the author believes that racial discrimination is harmful to both the white and the black people involved. Do you think that, even if discrimination of this kind did occur in the past, it no longer does so today – or, certainly, not in Great Britain? Write a paragraph explaining why you hold the view you do.

Glossary: **Of Mice and Men**

alfalfa: a kind of plant on which animals graze, similar to clover

ast: ask

averted: turned away

bindle: a blanket rolled up so that it can be carried easily across one's back, often with clothes and other possessons rolled up inside it; the word can also be used to refer to any package or bundle

bindle stiff: a hobo or tramp

blackjack: a card game

blowin' in our jack: losing our money

booby hatch: lunatic asylum

brighter 'n a bitch: very bright indeed

brush: undergrowth, brushwood

buck (barley, grain-bags, etc.): to carry or to throw

bullwhip: a long, plaited rawhide whip with a knotted end

bunk-house: sleeping quarters for ranch hands

burlap: a coarsely woven cloth made of fibres of jute, flax or hemp, and used to make sacks

can: to sack someone from a job

carp: a freshwater fish

cat-house: brothel

contorted: twisted

'coons: racoons, small wild animals related to the bear

'cots: apricots

derogatory: slighting, slightly scornful

disarming: charming

eatin' on: eating at, bothering

euchre: a card game

fawning: very anxious to please

fifty and found: fifty dollars a month pay, plus accommodation and food

figuring: doing sums, calculations with numbers

flats: stretches of sands sometimes submerged by water

floodwater wood: branches etc. carried down by a river in flood

floosie: stupid, worthless

goo-goos: people whose skin colour is not white

grey-backs: lice

grizzled: grey

halter: a device that fits around the head or neck of an animal and can be used to lead or secure it

hame: one of the two curved wooden or metal pieces of the harness that fit round the neck of an animal pulling a load, and to which the trace chains are attached

hoosegow: jail

horseshoe game: a game where the players throw horseshoes, with the aim of hitting or getting near a metal stake

jail bait: a woman with whom sexual involvement would lead to serious trouble. "Jailbait all set on the trigger" refers to a situation where there's clear opportunity for sexual involvement; and this involvement would almost certainly result in very bad trouble

jerkline skinner: a mule driver who uses long reins to control several animals

jungle-up: make a camp

kewpie doll lamp: a lamp that looks like a certain kind of doll – small, fat-cheeked and wide-eyed, with a curl of hair on top of the head

liniment: a thin ointment

morosely: gloomily

mottled: of blotched or smudgy appearance

nail-key: a small barrel for nails

pants rabbits: lice

pendular: a weight hung so that it can swing freely

poop: stamina, energy

poundin' their tail: working very hard

pulp magazine: cheap, popular magazine

punks: inexperienced young men

rabbit in: to run in

raptly: in an entranced way

rassel: heave

reprehensible: blameworthy

rigidly: stiffly

roaches: cockroaches

rummy: a card game

scourges: pests

skinner: a mule driver

slough: hit hard

solitare: the card game, patience, which is played by one person only

stable buck: ranch hand in charge of the animals and their equipment

stake: a comparatively large sum of money; an amount of money saved, borrowed or loaned to be used to start a new business

sullenly: in an angry, sulky way

swamper: odd-job man

ticking: a strong, tightly woven fabric of cotton or linen used especially to make pillow and mattress coverings

trace chains: one of two side chains connecting a harnessed animal to the vehicle it is pulling

two bits: a quarter (of a dollar) – 25 cents

vials: small containers for liquids

welter: welter-weight; a boxer over 10 stone (and not over 10 stone 8 pounds) (amateur)

wheeler: a wheel horse, the horse that follows the leader and is harnessed nearest to the front wheels

writhed: twisted

yammered: whined

yella-jackets: small wasps

The Pearl

Summary: The Pearl

John Steinbeck introduces his book with a prologue: that is, a few words telling us what kind of story we are about to read. We learn that the story is about the finding and losing of a great pearl and that the events in the story are very familiar to the people in the town where it all happened.

Chapter 1: pp. 7–18

Kino wakes up in the very early morning. As he lies in bed, his glance falls both on his wife, Juana, beside him and on the box where the baby, Coyotito, sleeps (p. 7). Juana gets up, checks that the baby is all right and then kindles the fire in preparation for making breakfast. While she does this, Kino gets up too and goes outside to watch the dawn (pp. 8–9).

Just as Kino and Juana have finished their breakfast inside the house, they see with horror that a scorpion is moving down the rope from which the baby's box hangs (p. 10). Juana prays silently while Kino glides towards the box; however, he is too late to prevent the insect from stinging Coyotito (p. 11). While the baby screams with pain, Juana sucks the poison out of the wound. Neighbours crowd into the house to see what is happening. Juana says that the doctor must be fetched (p. 12). When the neighbours tell her that the doctor would not be willing to make a visit, Juana sets out to visit him herself, carrying the baby. She is followed closely by her husband and a crowd of neighbours (p. 13).

They leave their own poor quarter of the city and enter the prosperous part. Beggars and others follow to see what will happen (p. 14). When they arrive at the doctor's house, Kino becomes frightened and angry:

he knows that the doctor is of an enemy race (p. 15). He knocks at the gate and is met by a servant (p. 15). The doctor meanwhile is sitting up in bed, drinking hot chocolate amidst surroundings of some luxury (p. 16). When the doctor hears that it is only "a little Indian" at the door, he grows angry and sends the servant to see whether the visitor has any money to pay for treatment. Kino offers some small seed pearls but these are rejected, the servant telling Kino that the doctor has gone out (p. 17). Publicly shamed, Kino strikes the doctor's gate with his fist.

Chapter 2: pp. 19–26

We are shown how the town lies at a river mouth, and how part of the beach is lined by drawn-up canoes. Although it is still early in the day, there is a heat haze (p. 19). Kino and Juana come down to the beach and to Kino's canoe (p. 20). After Kino has put his simple diving gear into the canoe, Juana places the baby in the boat. She then gathers some seaweed which she applies, as a poultice, to Coyotito's wounded shoulder. Kino and Juana launch the canoe and approach the oyster bed where the other pearlers are already at work (p. 21). It is a famous oyster bed where many valuable pearls have been found in the past. Kino takes his diving-rock and his basket and slips under the water (p. 22).

Hoping against hope that this morning he will be lucky, Kino chooses the largest shells he can see (p. 23). He notices a very large oyster, partly open, and thinks that he sees the gleam of a pearl. He forces the oyster free from its rock and carries it up to the surface. Once in the canoe, he brings up his basket of oysters; Juana senses his excitement. After opening some small, pearl-less oysters, he turns to the large one (p. 24). With Juana encouraging him to open it, he does so – and finds "the greatest pearl in the world" (p. 25). Juana calls him over to look at the baby: the swelling has gone down, Coyotito will survive. Kino is overcome by emotion and screams out loud (p. 26).

Chapter 3: pp. 27–45

Throughout the town, news soon spreads about the discovery of the Pearl of the World (p. 27). Many of the people who hear the news – including the priest, the doctor and the pearl buyers – think immediately of how the discovery could benefit themselves (p. 28). All kinds of people develop an interest in Kino; but, at the same time, hostility to, and envy of, the fisherman grows fast. Meanwhile, Kino and Juana, happy and excited, are congratulated by their relatives and neighbours (p. 29). When asked what he will do with his new wealth, Kino replies that he and Juana will be married in church; that the family will have new clothes; and that he himself will have a new harpoon and a rifle (p. 30). Highly excited, he says too that Coyotito will go to school (p. 31).

The neighbours realize that they are witnessing a very important event – but they are unsure whether it will end in good or evil (p. 32). As Juana begins to make preparations for dinner, the priest arrives to visit the family. Kino feels uneasy about this unexpected visitor who asks to see the pearl, but is unsure exactly where his unease lies (p. 33). The priest and the neighbours leave but, even against the familiar background of Juana preparing supper, Kino feels like a man set apart, eaten up by suspicions (p. 34). Aware that plans are dangerous things, Kino steels himself inwardly to make sure that he will overcome opposition to his dream for the future.

When the doctor and his servant arrive unexpectedly Kino receives them with partially concealed hatred (p. 35). Slyly, the doctor suggests that Coyotito may still suffer permanent injury from the scorpion's sting, and he offers to treat him to prevent this. Mistrustful but distressed, Kino allows the doctor to enter his house and look at the baby (p. 36). After persuading Kino that Coyotito is indeed still suffering from the effects of the sting, the doctor gives the baby a capsule of "medicine". He then leaves, warning that the baby will probably get worse within the hour but that he, the doctor, will return to save him (p. 37).

As he and Juana gaze anxiously at Coyotito, Kino notices that he still has the pearl in his hand. He goes and buries it in a corner of the dirt floor. Meanwhile, the doctor waits impatiently at home and the neighbours discuss the eventful day (p. 38). Kino has just finished his supper when Juana beckons him to look at the baby: Coyotito is vomiting (p. 39). The doctor returns to Kino's house, which is once again full of interested neighbours, and gives the baby a different kind of "medicine" (p. 40). Coyotito goes off to sleep and the doctor tries to find out about the pearl from a suspicious Kino. By the time the doctor leaves, he has managed to discover the probable hiding place of the pearl (p. 41).

Alone once again with his wife and child, Kino looks about outside the hut, then transfers the pearl from its earlier hiding place to a place under his sleeping-mat (p. 42). Kino wakes from an uneasy sleep to hear a soft rustling in a corner of his house. He springs on the intruder with his knife and in the ensuing scuffle Kino both delivers hurt and is hurt himself (p. 43). After Juana has tended his wounds, she tells Kino of her fear that the pearl is evil and will somehow destroy them all (p. 44). Kino refuses to accept her way of thinking and feeling and promises that in the morning, when he sells the pearl, all the evil will vanish (p. 45).

Chapter 4: pp. 46–62

Word soon spreads throughout the town that Kino is to sell his pearl on the day just commencing (p. 46); and the pearl buyers prepare themselves to make the most of their opportunity (p. 47). As the neighbours discuss how the future might turn out, Kino and Juana make sure that they look their best for the occasion (pp. 48–9). Followed by a crowd of neighbours, the family sets out to visit the pearl buyers.

As Kino walks at the head of the procession, he is advised by his brother, Juan Tomás, to take care not to be cheated by the pearl buyers (p. 50). The brothers agree that the history of their people shows how hard it is to avoid such a fate (p. 51). As the procession enters the stone-and-plaster city, the pearl buyers put the finishing touches to their offices and to their appearance (p. 52).

Kino brings the news of his find to the first buyer; and, according to plan, the buyer is careful to show no interest or excitement (p. 53). Even when he has actually seen the pearl, the buyer manages to keep up his act, trying to persuade Kino that the pearl has no great value (p. 54).

Kino protests angrily; and the buyer summons the other pearl buyers to give their opinions (p. 53). The other dealers put an even smaller value on the pearl than the first buyer (p. 56).

Kino snatches his pearl back from them and leaves, saying that he will sell his pearl elsewhere; the neighbours meanwhile disagree as to whether he has acted wisely (p. 57). Back in his house, Kino buries his pearl again and thinks hard about what to do next (p. 58). His brother warns him that he may be putting himself in great danger (p. 59). After sitting for some time in a near trance, Kino leaves the house (p. 60) and has a violent struggle with an attacker, resulting in a severe wound to Kino's head (p. 61). Juana tends his wound, then once again begs him to get rid of the pearl; again, Kino refuses to do this (p. 62).

Chapter 5: pp. 63–72

Kino awakes very late at night, and sees Juana removing the pearl from its hiding place. Silently, he follows her out to the shore. Just as she is about to hurl the pearl into the sea, he catches her arm, grasps the pearl, then strikes her in the face (p. 63). As he walks away from her, he is attacked by unseen assailants and, although he strikes back with his knife, the pearl is knocked from his hand. Juana, meanwhile, drags herself up from the beach (p. 64).

Finding the pearl in the path, she then sees two figures lying on the ground: one is Kino, the other a dead man (p. 65). She drags the corpse from the path and revives Kino with water; returning the pearl to him, she tells him that they now have no choice but to flee. Agreeing, Kino tells her to fetch the baby and some provisions; meanwhile, he finds that his canoe has had a large hole knocked in it (p. 66). Rushing back home, he sees that his house is on fire (p. 67). Juana comes running to meet him, carrying Coyotito in her arms, and tells him that intruders have ransacked the house, then set it alight.

Secretly, the family take refuge in the house of Juan Tomás nearby (p. 68). Once Juan Tomás has been told what has happened – and has been reassured that the family will not stay for long – he agrees to hide the fugitives (pp. 69–70). During the day, Juan Tomás borrows items useful to his brother; as evening approaches, Kino tells Juan Tomás that he intends to make for a city in the north (p. 71). After a formal farewell in the late evening, Kino and his family depart (p. 72).

Chapter 6: pp. 73–95

Kino and Juana leave La Paz, travelling north on foot (p. 73). They walk all night and in the dawn find a clearing near the road in which to rest (p. 74). Kino covers their tracks, has breakfast, and then discusses their situation with Juana (p. 75). After seeing the pearl – for the first time – as an evil influence on their lives, Kino sleeps a little (p. 76). When he awakes, he feels uneasy and, on surveying the road along which they have come, he sees three pursuing figures (p. 77).

Hiding by the side of the road, Kino prepares to defend himself against the pursuers (p. 78). Meanwhile, Juana keeps the baby quiet. The trackers pass the spot where the family is hiding; but Kino knows that they will come back. He returns to Juana (p. 79). Encouraged by his wife, Kino leads the family in a new direction – to the mountains (p. 80). The going is hard but Kino moves fast, in a panic of fear (p. 81). He tries to persuade Juana that it would be safer for them to travel separately; but she refuses to be parted from him (p. 82).

Eventually, the family arrives at a spring in the mountains where they can drink and rest a little (pp. 83–4). Having seen a number of small caves high up in the rock, Kino tells Juana that they must hide in one of these. Having first made a false trail, Kino joins his wife and son in a cave (p. 86). As the trackers arrive and settle down, Kino observes exactly how they position themselves (p. 87). He tells Juana that the family's only hope of safety lies in his attacking the pursuers while they rest. Reluctantly, she agrees and he prepares to do this (p. 88).

Climbing silently down the rock face (p. 89), Kino is caught out by the swift rise of the moon (p. 90). As he hides behind a bush, a cry comes from above and disturbs the resting men. Saying that a coyote pup may be making the noise, one of the men aims his gun; and is jumped on, mid-shot, by Kino with his knife poised to strike (p. 91). As the gun goes off, Kino stabs the gunman with his knife, then swiftly turns and finishes off the other two. But, when the killing is done, Kino hears Juana's wailing – wailing which means that the child is dead (p. 92).

Kino and Juana return to La Paz in the afternoon and are greeted by a large crowd. He carries a rifle, she the dead baby, and they ignore everyone and everything around them (p. 93). They walk straight through the city and on to the beach, where Kino offers the pearl to Juana. She refuses to take it; the next move is up to him. Kino then flings the pearl back into the sea (pp. 94–5).

Commentary: The Pearl

The prologue to the book tells us quite a lot about the nature of the story we are about to read. It is a story, it appears, that has been told many times before by the people in the town where the events occurred. What does John Steinbeck tell us happens to a story when it is told over and over again for a long time? Do you agree with him that what remains of the story is the meaning that all these different people have given to the events and the characters – that this one was good and that one was bad, and so on? Try to think of some other examples of this happening; you may decide, for example, that Westerns illustrate how stories can develop in this way.

You may have come across the word "parable" before in connection with certain stories in the New Testament of the Bible. It means 'a fable or story of something that might have happened, told to illustrate some particular way of looking at the world'. But John Steinbeck tells us that in the case of *The Pearl*, each person who hears the story will probably want to find his or her own meaning in it.

Chapter 1: pp. 7–18

On the first page of this chapter we are introduced to a man, Kino, and his family – his wife, Juana, and their baby, Coyotito. We see Kino in the process of waking up in the very early morning, watched, as always, by his wife. What kind of people do you think Kino and his wife are, and what kind of lives do they seem to live?

Already, on this first page, you'll see that we've been given a good many clues. The names "Juana" and "Coyotito", for example, sound of Spanish origin. And what do you make of the fact that Kino and his family live in a "brush house" (a house built out of brushwood) near which is a "tuna clump" (a patch of prickly-pear bushes)? Note down what else we learn on this first page about the life of the family.

Your notes will probably include the information that Kino and his wife sleep on a mat on the floor; and that they come from a people who have an ancient tradition of making songs. So what can we conclude from everything we've learned so far? Well, we already know from the prologue that Kino is a fisherman; we can now guess, in addition, that the family lives in a hot country (where solid houses are not so much needed, and where prickly-pears can grow) and is not wealthy (the simple house, and the sleeping-mat rather than bed). We know too that Kino's people is an ancient one with a strong cultural tradition and links with Spain. We can perhaps make a guess here that Kino and his family are Indians from Central or South America; these people, who included the Aztecs and the Incas, ruled Central and South America before the Spanish conquest in the sixteenth century.

We see, on p. 8, that Kino has his own song – the Song of the Family. If you've read the book through to the end, you'll know that soundless, internal, songs are very important to Kino; what do you think this might tell us about him? Have you ever felt music or a song inside you even though you made no sound? When might such a thing happen to you?

As Juana begins her preparations for the day, Kino goes outside to watch the dawn breaking over the Gulf (we don't know yet which Gulf this is). Note down the different things that Juana does. How do her activities differ from your own morning routine or that of your family?

Sitting outside the house, Kino can see the world coming awake and he can hear from inside the house the sounds Juana makes as she goes about her tasks. Note down what we are told about Kino's physical appearance. How would you describe his attitude to the life around him? Would you agree that from what we have seen so far this seems a calm and happy family?

Kino and Juana have a simple breakfast, as usual; we now know definitely that there is little room for luxury in their lives. They don't speak to each other very much, but the author comments that their silence doesn't indicate any discontent. In your experience, does silence between two people usually indicate that they're happy or unhappy with each other? How are you able to tell what kind of silence it is?

Once Kino and Juana have seen the scorpion approaching the baby's box, events move rapidly. This is a list of some of the things that happen; put them in the correct order:

1. Coyotito laughs and reaches out his hand.
2. Kino stretches out his hand.
3. The baby is stung.
4. Juana mutters spells and prayers.
5. Kino freezes to the spot.
6. The scorpion falls into the box.
7. The song in Kino's head changes.
8. The scorpion stops moving and prepares its sting.
9. Kino grabs for the scorpion but misses it.
10. Kino destroys the scorpion.
11. Kino moves swiftly towards the box.
12. Kino stands still.
13. Coyotito shakes the rope.
14. The scorpion moves delicately down the rope.

Have you ever been in a situation where a baby or a young child was in sudden, serious danger? Where were you? What could you see, hear, feel? In what order did things happen? Write a short account of what happened.

The incident with the scorpion tells us some new things about both Kino and Juana. Can you suggest what some of these might be? Have you included in your list the fact that, in the stress of the moment, Juana turns to the old magic of her people as well as to Christian prayer? And the fact that Kino is capable of terrible anger in defence of his family?

Seizing the child, Juana starts to suck out the poison from the sting, spitting it away, of course, so that she won't be poisoned herself. Is sucking the wound a sensible thing to do, do you think? Why?

We now meet the neighbours for the first time. They are to play an important part in the story (do you remember from the prologue that it is their children and grandchildren who have kept the story alive?), so pay careful attention to what they say and do. As we go on, you'll find that Kino and Juana live in a very close-knit community where no one approaches life in a spirit of minding his or her own business...

The neighbours fear that the baby may die as a result of the sting. Why should the scorpion be more harmful to a baby than to an adult?

Now look, on p. 12, at Kino's reflections on his wife. Make notes on how she appears to him and the contradictions which he finds in her.

What is the neighbours' first reaction to the news that Juana wants the doctor to be sent for? What kind of man do you suspect that this doctor may be? Why do you think this? Once Juana has made her decision to go and visit the doctor, the neighbours follow on behind the family.

As the procession passes from the simple, brush houses to "the city of stone and plaster", we begin to see a different way of living to the simple, basic life led by Kino and Juana. Think for a moment about the town or city where you live – or the one nearest to you; can you identify areas in it equivalent to the "brush houses" and "the city of stone and plaster"?

As the procession is joined by newcomers from the town, we learn more about the character of the doctor. The beggars, in particular, are familiar with this man; what do they know about him, and how have they found this out? Once the procession arrives at the doctor's large house, Kino hesitates for a moment. What mixture of feeling sweeps over Kino at this point, and why does he feel this way? Although the servant who opens the door is of Kino's own race, he refuses to speak to him in their own language; suggest some reasons for his behaving in this way. We now meet the doctor for the first time. He is plump and rich, it seems, but, unlike Kino and Juana in their normal circumstances, he is not happy. What kind of discontent does the doctor suffer from?

The servant tells the doctor that "a little Indian" is waiting outside; and we can now conclude for certain that the story is set in Central or South America where the Indians, the native race, were defeated and subsequently oppressed by their white, Spanish conquerors. The doctor soon makes it clear that he shares his race's contempt for the Indians; explain what the doctor means when he says (p. 17): "I am a doctor, not a veterinary." After the doctor has instructed his servant to ask if the waiting people have any money, the servant puts this question to Kino in their shared language; what do you think is the significance of this change?

When Kino's seed pearls are rejected, and an obvious lie is told about the doctor's movements, the crowd of people quickly thins away. What kind of "shame" has come over them? How does Kino react to his rejection by the doctor?

Chapter 2: pp. 19–26

Having seen two areas of the town in some detail – the brush houses and "the city of stone and plaster" – we are now given more of a bird's-eye view of the town's location. It lies, it seems, on a river mouth, and its buildings come right down to the beach. Canoes are lined up on the beach – canoes which provide Kino's people with the means of earning a living. Mention of the place name "Nayarit" confirms for us that the story is set in Mexico – and so we now know too that the "Gulf" mentioned earlier is probably the Gulf of California, lying to the west of the country. You may find it interesting and helpful at this point to look at a map of Mexico.

Read the description of the beach on p. 19, making notes on all the different things that can be seen; then think of a beach that you know well and write a paragraph describing what can be seen there. Note particularly the differences between the two beaches. On p. 20, John Steinbeck tells us of the effects of constant heat hazes on the attitudes of the people who live with them. Make notes on some of the main effects he describes.

Kino and Juana come to the beach and approach Kino's canoe; it is an important object in their lives and has a good deal of history behind it. Can you think of any object in your own or your parents' lives which is similarly important? Once Kino's diving gear is placed in the canoe, Juana lays the baby in it too, first having applied a poultice of seaweed to his shoulder. We're told that Juana has little confidence in this treatment of hers, although it is a sensible and appropriate way to deal with the baby's injury. Why does Juana have so little confidence in her treatment?

The canoe is launched and soon approaches the oyster bed. Have you ever seen an oyster bed? If not, is John Steinbeck's description of one different from what you thought an oyster bed might look like? In what ways? How had the oyster bed "raised the King of Spain to be a great power in Europe"? After first making notes, write a paragraph on how pearls come to be formed within oysters.

Kino slips into the water, carrying his diving-rock and his basket. What will each of these items be used for, do you think? As he collects oysters underwater, a new song fills his head – the Song of the Undersea. What kind of song is this? And what is the other song that is contained within this song? Why is this other song so clear on this particular day?

Kino suddenly sees a very large oyster lying by itself; and he catches sight of a gleam within the oyster. What is his immediate reaction to this sight? When he climbs into the canoe, Juana realizes at once that Kino is excited but she makes no outward sign. Why is she so cautious in her reactions? Having first opened the small oysters and found them pearl-less, Kino turns to the large shell. What goes through his mind at this point? When he does open the oyster, what does he find?

Kino sees "dream forms" in the surface of the pearl – but the hand in which he is holding the pearl is the hand that he hurt when he struck the doctor's gate. Would you agree that John Steinbeck is suggesting here that it is dangerous to overestimate the distance between dreams and reality?

When Juana goes to look at the baby, she finds that the swelling on his shoulder has gone down and that Coyotito seems to be out of danger. How does Kino react to this discovery? Why does he react in this way, do you think?

Chapter 3: pp. 27–45

John Steinbeck begins this chapter with a vivid description of how news can travel with great speed through a town. Have you ever known such a thing to happen in your city, town or village, or in a place well known to you? What was the event that sparked it off and how did the news spread from person to person?

Look at the following list of characters and then make notes on how each of these reacts to the news of the finding of the pearl:

1. The priest
2. The shop-keepers
3. The doctor
4. The beggars
5. The pearl buyers

Notice one thing in particular that we learn about the pearl buyers: that they are not in fact the separate buyers they appear to be but rather are agents for one main buyer. This means that the prices offered to the fishermen for the pearls they bring are controlled by one person alone; and this situation will inevitably result in very low prices indeed being offered.

Although different people have different dreams connected with the pearl, in most cases they have one thing in common: they resent Kino's good luck and come close to hating him for it. The author comments that, "The essence of pearl mixed with essence of men and a curious dark residue was precipitated" (p. 29). If you've studied any chemistry, you'll recognize the metaphor being used here: John Steinbeck is identifying both the attributes of the pearl and the human qualities of the people interested in it as chemical substances which, when mixed together, produce a different, dark substance. You'll notice that he continues this metaphor when, later in the paragraph, he uses the word "distillate" – that is, the product of the chemical process of distilling. He changes his metaphor in the next sentence when he writes of "poison sacs" beginning to manufacture "venom"; which living creature is he thinking of here, do you think?

Unaware of the darkness of spirit descending on the town, Kino and Juana celebrate their luck with joyful relatives and friends. When asked what he will do now that he has become a rich man, Kino gazes into the pearl; does it strike you here that, just as when he first set eyes on it, Kino is using the pearl almost as a crystal ball to assist looking into the future? What are the different things that Kino sees in his 'crystal ball'? Did you notice how Kino's thoughts quite overrun his words? Just look, for example, at the wealth of detail that lies behind these words of his, "We will have new clothes."

After the most important thing – the marriage in church – Kino turns to thinking of other, smaller things that he wants: a new harpoon, for example, and a rifle. Imagine for a moment that you have suddenly become very rich; what is the most important thing that you want and what are the smaller things? Now put yourself in your parents' or friends' shoes; what would they want, do you think? (You could try asking them to see if you're right.)

As Kino sees himself holding a rifle – a hitherto unimaginable idea – other equally 'impossible' dreams follow. Do you agree with the author when he comments that the reluctance of human beings to be satisfied with what they've got "is one of the greatest talents the species has"?

Give some examples to support your point of view. Kino's dreams, you'll probably have noticed, are far from being selfish ones: they're nearly all concerned with his family and his community. Write a paragraph describing and explaining the strong feeling expressed by Kino in the words, "My son will go to school."

Kino is rather frightened by his rush of thoughts; what kind of fear is he experiencing, do you think? Have you ever felt fear of a similar kind? In what circumstances did this happen? The neighbours react to his words rather differently: they know that they're very important but they're not sure as yet whether they'll end in spectacular success or catastrophic disaster. Prudently, they decide to wait and see. Have you ever come across a similar attitude on the part of friends or neighbours? If so, how did you feel about this attitude, and why did you feel this way?

As the evening draws in and Juana starts preparations for dinner, word spreads that the priest is coming. How do the people in the house react to his arrival? Why do they behave in this way? The priest, we are told, considers Kino and his people children – and treats them like children. Re-read the section describing the priest's approach to Kino and note down any evidence to support what we have been told. How does Kino react to the priest's words? What is the significance of the fact that, although the song in Kino's head has suddenly become the music of evil, Kino's first thought is to blame a neighbour for this rather than the priest?

When the priest leaves and, shortly afterwards, the neighbours go too, Juana continues her preparations for dinner and Kino goes outside. He is in an unusually suspicious and dark mood; did you notice how, unlike his behaviour in the early morning, he ignores the dog that approaches him? What lies behind this change in Kino? Write a paragraph explaining what is going on in his mind; you'll probably want to include, for example, the fact that he now realizes that he has enemies.

Kino sees two men approaching his house. What happens to him when he realizes who they are? The doctor clearly is not expecting a friendly reception but you'll probably agree that he has taken some care to plan his opening remarks. Do you think that Kino believes the doctor when he explains that he was not there when Kino came to his house? If not, why does Kino answer him with some degree of politeness? Have you ever been polite to someone you despised and hated? Why?

The doctor goes on to throw doubt on the completeness of the baby's recovery from the scorpion sting. He tells Kino that in some cases, after apparent improvement, the victim will have a sudden relapse and may end up with permanent injury to some part of his or her body. He suggests too that he, the doctor, can ensure that this will not happen in Coyotito's case. What trick does the doctor use to support these words of his? Why is this trick effective? Do you think that the doctor is speaking the truth? Why do you hold this view?

As happened earlier in the morning when he was faced with the prospect of dealing with this man of alien race, Kino is overcome by a mixture of feelings. Re-read the paragraph in the middle of p. 36 and then make notes on exactly what these feelings are and the order in which he feels them. Why does Kino decide in the end to allow the doctor to see Coyotito?

Juana's first reaction to the sight of the doctor is the same as Kino's: she wants to shield the baby from him. But, Kino having indicated that the doctor should see the baby, she passes him to the doctor. After examining Coyotito the doctor announces that the poison has indeed gone inwards and will strike soon; as proof, he shows Kino that the baby's eyelid is blue. At this point you may want to find a baby who hasn't recently been stung by a scorpion and check the colour of their closed eyelid . . .

The doctor fills a capsule with a white powder and gives it to the baby, saying that he will return in an hour – the time when he expects the poison to strike again. As Juana anxiously gazes at the baby, Kino discovers that he is still holding the pearl; he proceeds to bury it in a corner of the house. Meanwhile, the doctor settles back in his own house and waits; what do you think he is waiting for exactly? In their own houses, the neighbours discuss events so far and speculate on how riches will affect Kino and Juana. What opinion do the neighbours hold of the doctor? Do you think that their judgement is correct in this case?

Re-read the paragraph beginning, "Out in the estuary . . ." at the bottom of p. 38. Although John Steinbeck is here describing the activities of fish and, later, of mice and hawks, you may feel that what you're reading is also relevant to the human story we've been following. Write a paragraph explaining how the different things are connected.

In a frightened voice, Juana calls Kino to look at the baby and they both see that sickness has indeed come to him. How does Kino react to the baby's sudden illness? What are the suspicions that he feels? Meanwhile, the doctor looks at his watch and sets out for Kino's house. Word of the baby's illness has spread among the neighbours and, once again, they crowd into Kino's house. How do the neighbours react to the illness? Note down how their reaction differs from the reaction of the doctor earlier that morning.

The doctor arrives at the house and examines and treats the baby once more. Does the doctor's confidence allay Kino's suspicions? How does Juana react when the baby is declared to be out of danger? Do you think that the doctor was hoping that Kino would react in the same way? At last, the doctor manages to get the conversation round to the subject that we may suspect really interests him: the pearl that Kino has found. What trick does the doctor use to find out where Kino has hidden the pearl?

When the doctor and neighbours have gone, Kino remains alert to his surroundings, inside and out. He feels that all is not well, but you'll probably agree that he can't pinpoint the danger. Have you ever felt like this? Under what circumstances? As a precaution, Kino changes the hiding place of the pearl. Why is it, do you think, that when Kino eventually goes to sleep, he dreams of Coyotito reading a book?

Awakening in the dark, Kino has a song of evil ringing in his head; he hears a faint movement, waits a little, then springs on the intruder, striking out with his knife. What is the effect created by the author's describing the intruder as a "dark thing" rather than as a particular man? Would you agree that it both helps to put us, the readers, in Kino's place and creates an atmosphere of great menace?

Kino is hurt in the fight; but you'll probably agree that he is more badly hurt in his spirit and mind than in his body. Why might you think this? For the first time, Juana now expresses her strong feeling that the pearl is evil. Why do you think she feels this? Make a list of the bad things that have happened since Kino found the pearl. What is Kino's reaction to her words? Who do you suspect will be proved right? (Did you note particularly Juana's prophetic words at the very bottom of p. 44?)

The chapter closes with Kino once again gazing into the pearl and seeing and hearing marvellous things. Would you agree that he seems to be almost under a spell? What kind of spell do you think it is?

Chapter 4: pp. 46–62

Once again, we see how news spreads quickly in a small town – and we learn that the town where the action takes place is La Paz. You may find it interesting at this point to go back to your map of Mexico and look up La Paz. Now make a list of the different people in the town who learn that this is the day on which Kino intends to sell his pearl.

Re-read the paragraph on p. 47 beginning, "It was supposed that . . ." Why is it that the system was changed so that the pearl buyers no longer work as individuals acting alone? Was this change in the interests of the fishermen? If not, who did benefit from the change? How would you describe the tone of voice used by the author in this passage? Would you agree that when he says things like, "This was extravagant . . .", he is being *ironic* – that is, he is conveying the opposite of what the words actually mean? John Steinbeck, we may be sure, does not think it right that the fishermen should be paid rock-bottom prices for their pearls. This kind of irony is quite often used in ordinary conversation; can you think of any examples that you have heard recently?

As usual, the neighbours suspend their ordinary lives in order to follow the development of the big news story – Kino and his pearl. In discussing it all, they come up with several ideas on how they themselves would spend the money had they been the ones to strike lucky. Note down what these different ideas are. What do the neighbours fear may happen to Kino and Juana? Why do they fear this, do you think?

It is a momentous day for Kino and Juana and they dress up in their simple best. Leaving when the sun is "quarter high" (that is, early in the morning when the sun has travelled only a quarter of its distance up the sky), Kino and Juana once again head a procession to the city. Kino is careful to wear his straw hat in a particular way; what impression is he trying to give? Is there any item of clothing that you tend to wear with particular care? What impression are you hoping to create by doing this?

Leading the procession with his brother, Juan Tomás, Kino listens to some words of advice. What advice does Juan Tomás give his brother, and why does he feel that Kino needs it? Juan Tomás goes on to tell Kino a story about events that took place in the community before Kino was born. Using your own words, write an account of the story Juan Tomás tells; then make notes on what you think happened to the agents who set out for the capital. Why do you think Juan Tomás has chosen this moment to tell the story to Kino? Kino responds to the story by giving the priest's explanation of the events; what is this explanation?

Re-read the paragraph on p. 51 beginning, "The brothers, as they walked along . . ." Would you agree that what John Steinbeck is conveying here is a sense that Kino and his brother, like the rest of their people, are suspicious and wary of anything told to them by people from the conquering white race? Do you think that they're right to be suspicious? If so, why do you think this?

As the procession grows and approaches the street where the pearl buyers have their offices, the buyers prepare themselves carefully for the visitor who may come. What kind of preparations do they make, and why? Since we are given a close view of one man in particular, we can safely assume that this is the one whom Kino will choose to visit first. Many of the words that are used to describe him are quite positive ones – "benign" and "jolly", for example; but what is your overall impression of the kind of man this is? You may well agree that on the whole he doesn't seem to be a person whom one would readily trust. Look carefully at the description on pp. 52–3 of his "legerdemain" (that is, his juggling, his sleight-of-hand); then write a paragraph explaining why this description might make you suspicious of the buyer's outward appearance.

The pearl buyer is anxious to convey the impression that Kino's pearl is a matter of indifference to him; why does he want to do this? Even when he has seen the pearl, he manages to keep up the pretence that acquiring it is not of great importance to him. Why does he think that he will be able to persuade Kino that his pearl is not the "Pearl of the World"? When Kino shows no sign of giving in to him, the buyer suggests that he, Kino, should ask the opinion of the other dealers; and the buyer immediately sends for these men. Unlike Kino's friends and Kino himself, we know that this consultation will not help Kino at all; what do we know about the pearl buyers that Kino and his friends don't? Kino and his neighbours have very different reactions to the pearl buyer's valuation of the pearl; make notes on the main differences.

The other three dealers arrive and give their valuations of the pearl. Taking each dealer in turn, make notes on how they judge Kino's pearl. (Note particularly how the second dealer tries to pull the same trick on Kino as did the doctor earlier: that is, almost literally 'to blind him with science'.) Can you see what the dealers are aiming to do by taking this approach? When Kino angrily refuses the best price offered, the dealers realize that they have misjudged their man. What kind of misjudgement have they made?

That evening, the neighbours sit in their brush houses and discuss the events of the morning. Once again, they are divided in their opinions. Write a paragraph describing the main opinions expressed. Which opinion do you suspect that the author is most in sympathy with? Which opinion do you agree with?

In his own house, Kino sits brooding, having once again changed the hiding place of the pearl. What does the author mean, do you think, when he says, "He had lost one world and had not gained another"? Have you ever felt in between "worlds"? When and how did this happen?

Juan Tomás comes to discuss matters with Kino; but you'll probably agree that he hasn't much comfort or support to offer. Indeed, he even introduces some new worries and concerns; what are these? Feeling even more depressed after his brother has gone, Kino sits almost in a trance, the song in his head overwhelmingly one of evil. Always the dutiful wife, Juana waits for him to re-enter their life. Instead, Kino responds to some silent call from outside – and steps straight into a vicious attack.

You'll probably have noticed by now that one of the things John Steinbeck is trying to do in this book is to convey the thinking and behaviour of people who are not educated, who live very close to nature and who, on the whole, are not much given to talking and discussion. How successful is he, do you think, in doing this? What are the main ways in which he tries to give us a sense of how Kino and his people experience the world?

After Juana has given Kino first aid for his injuries, she implores him once again to get rid of the pearl. How does Kino respond to her entreaties?

Chapter 5: pp. 63–72

Kino wakes in the dark and sees Juana take the pearl from its hiding place and then leave the house. In great anger he follows her to the beach and snatches the pearl from her just as she is about to throw it into the sea. He then strikes and kicks her, before leaving her lying among boulders. This is a very different Kino to the one we have seen before; imagining for a moment that you are Kino, write a paragraph explaining why you behaved in this way. When you've finished, write a paragraph describing the same events – but this time from Juana's point of view. Remember to take into account what we're told about Juana on p. 64. Once you've finished this exercise, take a few moments to consider which viewpoint you feel most in sympathy with, and why.

Once again Kino is attacked by unknown assailants; but, this time, the consequences are very serious indeed – one of the attackers lies dead on the path. Although Kino was quite aware that he had wounded his attacker deeply, his first thought on regaining consciousness has nothing to do with the victim. What is his first concern, and what does this tell us about his state of mind? (You may feel that you want to refer back to some of the things you've just written when imagining Kino's point of view.)

Juana understands very clearly the implications of what has happened and, with her support, Kino soon pulls himself together. Telling her to fetch Coyotito and some provisions, he goes to prepare the canoe for their escape. When he discovers that the boat has been holed, a number of different strong emotions sweep over him. Note down the different emotions which Kino feels; then write a paragraph explaining why he feels these things.

On running back to his house, Kino finds that it is ablaze. Juana tells him that "the dark ones" have destroyed the house; why does she use these words, do you think, and what were these people hoping to achieve? Suddenly afraid of the light, Kino himself begins to share at least one of the qualities of "the dark ones". Note down at this point some of the main changes that have taken place in Kino's behaviour and attitudes since we met him first. Do you think that these changes prove that Juana was right to give such strong warnings about the effects of the pearl on their lives?

Taking refuge in the house of Juan Tomás, Kino and his family allow the other neighbours to think that they have been killed in the fire. Juan Tomás is very disturbed to hear about the latest events in Kino's life and, a little reluctantly, agrees to let the family stay hidden for a short time. Why does Juan Tomás hesitate in giving his agreement, do you think?

While Kino and his family stay silent and hidden, Juan Tomás spreads a number of rumours about them among the neighbours. Note down the rumours that he spreads; then write a couple of sentences explaining why he has done this. At the same time, Juan Tomás manages to borrow some items useful to the family in their flight. If you were in great danger and had to run away from your town, what items would you want to take with you? You'll probably find that your list is very different to Kino's; why is this?

Kino tells Juan Tomás that he still has the pearl; but you'll notice that his attitude to this has changed very much indeed. Would you agree, for example, that Kino now sees the pearl as a burden to be endured rather than as a piece of good fortune to be celebrated? Taking into account also what Kino says about the pearl on p. 72, what other changes would you note?

After darkness has fallen, the family leave for their perilous trip to the city in the north. Judging by the author's account of the farewell between the brothers, do you think that they are hopeful about the success of the trip?

Chapter 6: pp. 73–95

The wind high, the family walk round the outskirts of the town, out into the open country. Why is the high wind a good thing from their point of view? They take the road to Loreto (perhaps you'd like to take a quick look at an atlas here), a town celebrated for its association with a miraculous apparition of the Virgin Mary. (The word "station" on p. 73 refers to the much visited place where this event occurred; it also carries echoes of the phrase 'Stations of the Cross', meaning the representations of stages in Christ's way to Calvary found in many Roman Catholic churches.)

As usual, Juana walks behind Kino. Kino himself is full of nervous energy and excitement. Have you ever felt emotions similar to those described at the bottom of p. 73? Under what circumstances? The wind drops eventually, but the family walk on. Have you ever walked all through the night? After re-reading the description on p. 74 of the sounds the family hears, note down the different sounds that you heard — or imagine that you would hear — on an all-night walk near to where you live.

In the silence of the family's flight, the grand music of the pearl reasserts itself in Kino's head, in harmony with the song of the family. Would you agree that Kino has found hope again – that he still believes, deep down, that the pearl will eventually bring them all happiness?

At dawn, they find a clearing by the road in which to rest; and Kino makes sure that their footprints are removed from the road. While Juana sleeps, Kino thinks about their situation; what message do you think he takes from the behaviour of the ants described on p. 75? Look at the advice he gives Juana at the bottom of that same page; if you were in a clearing in the countryside near where you live, what kind of advice and warnings would you give to a companion?

As husband and wife talk, the conversation inevitably turns to the pearl and its implications for their lives. Do you remember how Kino had earlier used the pearl almost as a crystal ball in which to see the future? Here we see this process in reverse. When Kino looks into the pearl, hoping for inspiration, this time he finds dreadful images from the past. Note down the things that he sees and contrast them with the things he saw before. Do you think that the change lies in the pearl itself or in Kino?

Kino sleeps while Juana plays with the baby. When he wakes up, he is uneasy, although there is no suspicious sound to be heard. You'll probably agree that his senses are so stretched through fear that he has acquired some of the acute sensitivities of an animal. His wariness is proved justified when he looks along the road and sees three faraway figures moving in his direction. Two of them he identifies as trackers (that is, men skilled in following the traces, however slight, of a living creature); the third is on horseback and carries a rifle.

As the figures draw nearer, Kino decides what action to take if the family's hiding place is discovered. What does he plan to do – and do you think it a good plan? Do you think that, in similar circumstances, you would show as much presence of mind as Kino does? Juana too, you'll probably agree, thinks and acts pretty quickly in silencing Coyotito.

The family is lucky this time; after some hesitation, the men move on. But Kino knows how thorough they are, and he knows that they will come back. Have you ever taken part in laying or following trails? What did you find difficult about it? Did you find it exciting?

When Kino returns to Juana he has lost his determination and presence of mind. Once again, Juana puts new heart into him; do you remember her doing this before, soon after she herself has been struck by him? It clearly would be a mistake to think of Juana as a woman guided only by her husband, with no will of her own.

Heading for the mountains, the family flees first through undergrowth, then across desert country. Have you ever walked across country where rain rarely falls? In what ways was it similar to, and different from, the country described on p. 81? What kind of music sounds in Kino's head as he moves towards the mountains?

They stop to rest a little as the land rises, and find that their pursuers are nowhere in sight. Kino tells Juana to take the baby and go north alone; he himself will continue on to the mountains. But Juana steadfastly refuses. Why does Kino want Juana to go on alone, do you think? And why does Juana refuse? Do you think that they have come to the right decision in the end?

Once again taking pains to cover their tracks, Kino and Juana move closer to the mountain range. Why do they decide to head for a particular cleft ('cleft' meaning an opening, a crack) in the mountain range? What might be the dangers associated with this destination? Re-read, from the bottom of p. 83 to the top of p. 85, John Steinbeck's description of this cleft and the spring which it contains. If you like drawing, you may find it helpful to sketch the scene which the author describes; otherwise, make notes describing the different kinds of wildlife, animals and plants, which find sanctuary by the streams and pools.

Arriving at a pool on a stone platform within the cleft, the family refresh themselves a little. But when Kino looks out over the horizon, he sees that the pursuing men are on their trail. What plan does Kino then form for avoiding capture? Note down the different actions that he takes in carrying out his plan and explain the purposes of the different actions involved. The family then begin their long wait in the cave until the trackers reach the pool – the wait being a long one partly because Kino has already been so successful in laying false trails.

When the pursuers eventually arrive at the pool, they behave as if they are quite taken in by the false trail left by Kino. However, they make no move to follow on immediately; instead they drink, eat and rest by the pool. Although it is soon quite dark, Kino gets a clear sighting of how the three men are positioned; how does he manage to do this?

Crawling back into the cave, Kino tells Juana what he intends to do now that his earlier plan has fallen through. Continuing to hide in the cave till the pursuers leave is not possible, he says, because the morning light will reveal the family's hiding place. What does Kino see as the only possible means of escape from their very dangerous situation? How does Juana respond to his whispered words? Imagining that you are Kino bidding farewell to his family, write a paragraph describing your feelings and thoughts.

Having first taken off his clothes (why does he do this?), Kino attaches his knife to the cord he wears round his neck (an "amulet" is a charm to ward off evil spirits) and disappears from Juana's view. Once again, Juana whispers "her combination of prayer and magic". Do you remember an earlier occasion when she did this? Were her prayers answered on that occasion?

In the darkness, Kino climbs down the rockface, taking great care to be absolutely silent. What is the music sounding in his head during the climb? You'll probably agree that the description of the climb on pp. 89–90 is very vivid and exciting; note down two ways in which John Steinbeck has managed to communicate the excitement and tension of Kino's climb. As Kino prepares himself to spring on the man on watch, the moon rises; why does this prevent Kino from making his move?

As Kino waits for his next chance to attack, a whimpering cry breaks the silence. What do Kino's enemies think may be the source of the sound? What is the realization that makes Kino break into a sweat? Events now move only too quickly. As Kino leaps for the man with the rifle, the gun is fired. Knifing the gunman, Kino then seizes the rifle and makes short work of the remaining two men. Are you surprised by the ferocity of his attack? Write a paragraph explaining your answer to that question.

On p. 92 John Steinbeck writes, "Kino's brain cleared from its red concentration." What do you understand by the phrase, "red concentration"? Make some suggestions as to why it is such a vivid phrase in the context. What is the significance of the sound that Kino hears once he has come out of his warlike trance? Who is uttering the cry of death, and whose death is the cause of the cry?

For most of this chapter, we have seen the action directly; it's almost as if we have been accompanying Kino and Juana on their flight from the city. But we see their return to La Paz much more indirectly – once again, as earlier in the story, entering the action through the viewpoint of the people of the town. Would you agree that this change has the effect of distancing the figures of Juana and Kino, making them once again, as they were in the prologue, figures of legend, larger than life? What other effects does the change have on your perception of the pair?

Now write a paragraph contrasting the way in which the family returns to the town with the way they left it. Remember to mention such things as the fact that Juana no longer walks behind Kino – and the fact that Juana still carries Coyotito, but in a gruesomely different way to the way she carried him before.

Walking straight through the town and paying no attention to any of the landmarks of their recent history, Kino and Juana come to the water's edge. What does Kino see in the pearl when he looks into it for the last time? How do you think he feels as he sees these pictures? Make notes now, suggesting, first, why Kino offers the pearl to Juana and, second, why Juana insists that he perform the final action.

Our last glimpse of the pearl is touched with beauty. Think for a moment about why John Steinbeck might have decided to present it in this way. Would you agree that it may well be because all the ugliness associated with the pearl has come from the meaning attached to it by human beings; but the undersea world has no such meanings in it?

Characters: The Pearl

Do you remember what John Steinbeck says in the prologue to his book – that "as with all retold tales that are in people's hearts, there are only good and bad things and black and white things and no in-between anywhere"? After having read *The Pearl*, you may well feel that there is a great deal of truth in this as far as the characters are concerned. On the whole, the characters are fairly unambiguously good or bad, innocent or evil; we nearly always know whose side we're supposed to be on.

However, you'll probably agree that there is just enough ambiguity, just enough uncertainty at times to deepen our interest in some of the characters. We're never quite sure about the neighbours, for example. Sometimes, we're given the impression that they're wholeheartedly on the side of Kino and Juana; at other times, it's suggested that their actions and attitudes will be influenced most heavily by considerations to do with their personal comfort and safety. And then there is Kino himself. Let's now take a closer look at the fisherman, along with the two other main characters – Juana and the doctor.

KINO

Because Kino is perhaps the most central character in the story, it's not possible to get a full view of what kind of person he is just by reading a few selected sections of the book. We can get to know Kino only by paying careful attention throughout the book both to how we see him behave and to what is said about him.

We first meet Kino in a state of apparent great content; he lives very simply but it doesn't occur to him to wish for a more luxurious life. The illness of Coyotito and Kino's subsequent encounter with the doctor provoke in the fisherman the first stirrings of resentment, hatred and fear. These feelings are aroused even more strongly by the events that occur after Kino has found the pearl. Note down some examples of aggression and contempt shown towards Kino by other characters. In your opinion, does Kino continue to keep possession of the pearl because he is anxious to have all the things that money can buy, or because his blood is up as a result of being insulted, cheated and attacked?

Although you may well feel that Kino behaves as he does largely because of the way he has been treated, there's no doubt that at some points in the story he is quite bewitched by the pearl and what it represents to him. Note down the main things that the pearl does represent to Kino; having done that, you'll probably find that your list shows that he is far from being a selfish man. Would you agree that the most important thing for him seems to be the chance to provide Coyotito with an education? This chance, of course, goes for ever with the rifleshot in the mountains; in the end, the only gift given to the child by the pearl is a violent death.

As Kino's brother says, he, Kino, has "defied not the pearl buyers, but the whole structure, the whole way of life" (p. 59). Do you think that because the episode of the pearl ends in disaster, John Steinbeck wants us to look on Kino as a rash and misguided man? Or do you think that the story provides a picture of a brave man who comes to learn about human evil in the hardest way possible?

JUANA

Like Kino, Juana figures prominently throughout the book. However, you may find it helpful to re-read at this point some sections which focus directly on her: p. 12, pp. 63–6, p. 80, p. 82 and p. 94.

We first meet Juana performing the actions of a very dutiful and obedient wife and mother. However, we soon learn that, apparently fragile, she can display considerable strength when the occasion requires it. This strength, it turns out, is not confined to physical prowess: Juana also has great reserves of emotional and mental toughness. Write notes on two occasions when Juana shows particular emotional strength and clear-mindedness.

You'll probably have included at least one of the occasions when she jolts Kino into an awareness of the realities of their situation and the action that they must take to save themselves. Would you agree that throughout the book Juana shows much less tendency than Kino to day-dream and to avoid looking facts in the face?

Take a close look at the paragraph on p. 64 starting, "Juana dragged herself up . . ." What do you think about the views expressed here? Do you agree, for example, that men — but not women — are "half insane and half god"? And do you agree that there are such clear differences between men and women as those described here? Write a paragraph giving your own views on this subject, along with some explanation of why you hold those views.

THE DOCTOR

We learn about the doctor at four main points in the book: pp. 14–17, pp. 27–8, pp. 35–8, and pp. 40–41. Look through these sections again carefully before you read on.

Among the first things we learn about the doctor are that he is of an enemy race to Kino's people; and that, in comparison with them, he is immensely rich. His luxurious life, however, seems to bring him little happiness. There's a suggestion (on p. 16) that he married for money; and even the town's beggars know how incompetent he is as a doctor. The main driving force behind this character seems to be greed; and his greed reaches out to everything surrounding him. Note down some examples of the different kinds of greed displayed by the doctor.

The doctor's discontent with life is fuelled by idealized memories of his time in Paris. Do you know anyone who keeps harking back nostalgically to an earlier time, and constantly compares present circumstances unfavourably with past ones? Do you feel any sympathy with this person? If so, why? If not, why not?

Themes: The Pearl

Once again, let's look back at the prologue to *The Pearl*. "If this story is a parable," says John Steinbeck, "perhaps everyone takes his own meaning from it and reads his own life into it." In reading the book, you may well have found this to be true; and so you'll probably want to add your own choice of themes to those given below.

NATURE VERSUS CIVILIZATION

There are several layers of life portrayed in *The Pearl*. Think for a moment about what these are. Do your suggestions include the people who make their living by fishing and pearling; the town people who sell and buy; and the animals, birds and insects who pursue their own imperatives?

Let's look a little more closely at how these different layers of life relate to one another. You may find it helpful to think about them in terms of how close they are to the natural world. The animals, birds and insects are obviously contained almost entirely within the natural world – although we do see a 'civilized' dog which is much attached to Kino. The fisher people live harmonious lives very close to nature. They have to be very knowledgeable about the environment surrounding them, since they depend for their living on exploiting natural resources. They also live in brush houses and sleep close to the ground. The people of the town, on the other hand, live in, or near, a "city of stone and plaster"; and they have a second-hand relationship with the natural world. The pearl buyers, for example, see pearls only in terms of cash.

When Kino finds the pearl, he is suddenly hurtled from one layer of life into another; and many of his difficulties spring from his unfamiliarity with the customs and values of the "city of stone and plaster". What are some of these customs and values and what do you see as John Steinbeck's attitude towards them?

You'll probably agree that the author despises the greed and callousness displayed by many of the people of the town – including, to different degrees, the doctor, the priest and the pearl buyers. In theory more 'civilized' (because further from nature), these people in fact show very few of the qualities that one might like to think of as 'civilized' – for example, kindness and gentleness.

Now think for a moment about the author's portrayal of the natural world. Does he present this in an entirely rosy light in contrast to the hypocrisy and ruthlessness of the city? You'll probably agree that the answer to this is definitely 'no'; think about the episode of the scorpion, for example; or the description of the mountain cleft: "The little pools were places of life because of the water, and places of killing because of the water too" (p. 84).

Danger and violence are common to both the civilized and the natural world, he is perhaps implying; but the civilized world offers more to fear in the sense that the hand that strikes you may well just have shaken your hand in friendship.

INJUSTICE

Just as injustice forms an important theme of *Of Mice and Men*, so it echoes through *The Pearl*. Take a moment to note down the kinds of injustice that you see displayed in the story.

The first time we come across injustice directly in *The Pearl* is when we learn from the neighbours that the doctor is only interested in treating rich people. Would you agree that a society where poor people have no access to medical treatment can fairly be called unjust? Give reasons for your opinion.

We then go on to learn that the doctor comes from a race which for hundreds of years has oppressed and cheated Kino's race. Since we soon find out that Kino's people are Central American Indians, we can deduce that the doctor is of European origin. His remark on p. 17 – "Have I nothing better to do than cure insect bites for 'little Indians'?

I am a doctor, not a veterinary" – displays only too clearly his belief that his race is infinitely superior to Kino's. As his later conduct shows, the doctor has no concept of justice as far as the Indian people are concerned; he sees them only as servants to be exploited, animals to be ignored, or victims to be cheated and robbed. What do you see as John Steinbeck's attitude to this approach?

Think now about the approach to the Indian people taken by some other characters: the priest and the pearl buyers. Note down examples of injustice to be found in their behaviour and attitudes. Have you included a reference to the sermon delivered each year by the priest (p. 51)? You'll probably agree that this is an attempt to justify injustice. Have you ever heard or read of a similar case being put forward to justify a situation that you think of as unjust? How did you react to being presented with such arguments?

One of the ways in which John Steinbeck makes clear his hatred of the kinds of injustice discussed here is to contrast the behaviour of the 'superior' race with that of the 'inferior' one. Think, for example, of the occasion when, his canoe destroyed and his life in danger, Kino still doesn't even entertain the thought of taking a neighbour's boat (p. 67). His strong moral sense stands in sharp contrast with the unscrupulousness of the pearl buyers, the doctor and the other 'civilized' men. Note down some other examples of the Indian community displaying an acute sense of justice.

DREAMS VERSUS REALITY

Once again, we have a theme which is also important in *Of Mice and Men*. The focus for dreams in this story, of course, is the pearl itself – the Pearl of the World, as Kino calls it.

On p. 29 we see how nearly everybody in the town responds to the finding of the pearl by attaching their own dreams to it. Kino himself is quick to do the same – though, as we have seen, his dreams are remarkably unselfish ones. However, it soon becomes clear that even unselfish dreams are dangerous. The pearl is not just a beautiful object: it is a commodity with cash value – and, as such, it brings dreams and reality together in violent collision.

As Kino learns bitter lessons about 'civilized' behaviour, so the pearl itself, along with his dreams, becomes tarnished and dulled. As we see at several points in the story, Kino uses the pearl almost like a crystal ball, hoping to see a bright future reflected in it. But as events take an increasingly violent turn, so the dreams reflected in the pearl change into nightmares. Note down some examples of this happening.

What is John Steinbeck telling us about the relationship between dreams and reality? Well, first of all, he's perhaps suggesting that in a world full of greed and injustice the simple dreams of innocent people are unlikely to be easily fulfilled. Secondly, he may be implying that, as with Kino, a dream can assume a great power of its own, blinding the dreamer to the reality around him or her.

However, although these messages may be found in the story, an important question still remains. Is John Steinbeck suggesting that Kino should early on have given up hope of attaining his dream? Write a paragraph giving your answer to this question and explaining why you hold the view you do.

Glossary: **The Pearl**

algae: seaweed

amulet: a charm carried about the person

ant lion: a kind of insect which traps ants in a funnel-shaped sand-hole

avarice: eager desire for wealth; greed for gain

barnacle-crusted: covered with tight-clinging small animals often found on rocks or ships' bottoms

benign: kindly

bit-roller: part of the bridle that the horse wears in the mouth

bougainvillea: a plant, mainly tropical American, carrying purple flowers

braced: strengthened

brush houses: houses made of brushwood, broken branches, and so on

bulwark: a means of defence or security

cackled: made a sound like a hen or goose

cacti: cactuses, plants whose stems store water

chittered: chattered

cicada: an insect remarkable for its loud chirping sound

cleft: an opening made by splitting; a fissure or crack

colonial animal: a number of organisms living together in a community but forming one living creature

consecrated: set apart for holy use

countenanced: approved

covert: thicket, hidden place

covey: a small flock

cozened: cheated

crevices: cracks

crooning: singing in an undertone

curdled: clotted, thickened

dank: unpleasantly moist, wet

disparagement: in a dishonouring way, by comparing a superior with an inferior

dissembling: disguising, assuming a false appearance

distillate: the product of converting a liquid into vapour by heat, and then condensing again

edifice: a building; a large structure

escarpment: the steep side of a hill or rock

estuary: the wide lower tidal part of a river

exhilaration: great cheer and good spirits

feinted: made deceptive attacking movements

fiddler crab: a kind of crab which has an enlarged claw

fiesta: saint's day; holiday

freshet: a stream of fresh water; a flood

furtive: stealthy; secret

germane: related; appropriate

gourd: rind of a certain kind of plant which can be used as a bottle or cup

grinding-stone: a stone for grinding corn

guttural: throaty, deep

hammocks: hummocks; little hills

herring clouds: clouds shaped like a shoal of herring

hibiscus: a kind of tropical plant

illumined: made bright

inaudible: not able to be heard

incandescence: a white heat

indigene: a native person

indigent: in need

kelp: large brown seaweed

lateen: small triangular (sail)

legerdemain: sleight-of-hand; juggling

leprosy: a chronic and very serious disease of the skin

lucent: shining; bright

mangrove: a tree that grows in muddy swamps, tropical coasts and estuary shores

mirage: an appearance of objects in the sky owing to the effect of layers of hot and cold air

optical: relating to sight or to the eye

parable: a fable or story of something which might have happened, told to illustrate a particular way of looking at the world

participation: taking part in

pivoting: turning round and round on one spot

poultice: a soft composition applied in a cloth to sores or wounds

precipitated: brought down from a state of solution or suspension

pulque: a fermented drink made in Mexico from agave sap

pulsing: beating; throbbing

rampart: a flat-topped defensive mound

residue: that which is left

rigid: stiff; unbending

rupture: a breach, breaking or bursting

seed pearl: a very small pearl

skirled: shrieked

slat: a thin strip of wood

stalwart: strong; sturdy

station: a holy place visited as one of a series

strand: yarn or thread twisted with others to form a rope

subjugation: being under domination

suppliant: entreating, supplicating

swabbed: wiped clean with soft material

tithe: a small part

tule: a large American bulrush

tuna clump: a patch of prickly-pear bushes

ulcerous: ugly and poisoned-looking
undulating: moving like waves

venom: poison; spite
vibrate: to shake; to tremble

watered silk: silk marked with a wavy pattern as a result of watering
Winchester carbine: a short light musket produced by an American manufacturer

Passages for Comparison

OF MICE AND MEN

In this extract from the poem, 'The Ballad of Reading Gaol' (1898) by Oscar Wilde, we can sense the poet's strong feeling that human love all too often ends in disaster. Once you've read the piece, perhaps you'd like to take one of the situations he describes and write about it from the victim's point of view?

> Yet each man kills the thing he loves,
> By each let this be heard,
> Some do it with a bitter look,
> Some with a flattering word,
> The coward does it with a kiss,
> The brave man with a sword!
>
> Some kill their love when they are young,
> And some when they are old;
> Some strangle with the hands of Lust,
> Some with the hands of Gold:
> The kindest use a knife, because
> The dead so soon grow cold.
>
> Some love too little, some too long,
> Some sell, and others buy;
> Some do the deed with many tears,
> And some without a sigh:
> For each man kills the thing he loves,
> Yet each man does not die.

THE PEARL

In these short extracts from the novel *Nicholas Nickleby* (1839) by Charles Dickens, we see the development of a man whose love of money distorts his view of everything else in life. Once you've read the extracts, perhaps you would like to write an account of how such a man might feel in a lonely old age?

Extract A

With a portion of this property [inherited from an uncle] Mr Godfrey Nickleby purchased a small farm near Dawlish in Devonshire, whither he retired with his wife and two children, to live upon the best interest he could get for the rest of his money, and the little produce he could raise from his land. The two prospered so well together that, when he died, some fifteen years after this period, and some five after his wife, he was enabled to leave, to his eldest son, Ralph, three thousand pounds in cash, and to his youngest son, Nicholas, one thousand and the farm, which was as small a landed estate as one would desire to see.

These two brothers had been brought up together in a school at Exeter; and, being accustomed to go home once a week, had often heard, from their mother's lips, long accounts of their father's sufferings in his days of poverty, and of their deceased uncle's importance in his days of affluence: which recitals produced a very different impression on the two: for, while the younger, who was of a timid and retiring disposition, gleaned from thence nothing but forewarnings to shun the great world and attach himself to the quiet routine of a country life, Ralph, the elder, deduced from the often-repeated tale the two great morals that riches are the only true source of happiness and power, and that it is lawful and just to compass their acquisition by all means short of felony. 'And,' reasoned Ralph with himself, 'if no good came of my uncle's money when he was alive, a great deal of good came of it after he was dead, inasmuch as my father has got it now, and is saving it up for me, which is a highly virtuous purpose; and going back to the old gentleman, good *did* come of it to him too, for he had the pleasure of thinking of it all his life long, and of being envied and courted by all his family besides.' And Ralph always wound up these mental soliloquies by arriving at the conclusion, that there was nothing like money.

Extract B

On the death of his father, Ralph Nickleby, who had been some time before placed in a mercantile house in London, applied himself passionately to his old pursuit of money-getting, in which he speedily became so buried and absorbed, that he quite forgot his brother for many years; and if, at times, a recollection of his old playfellow broke upon him through the haze in which he lived – for gold conjures up a mist about a man, more destructive of all his old senses and lulling to his feelings than the fumes of charcoal – it brought along with it a companion thought, that if they were intimate he would want to borrow money of him. So, Mr Ralph Nickleby shrugged his shoulders, and said things were better as they were.

Discussion Topics

Your understanding and appreciation of these stories will be much increased if you discuss aspects of them with other people. Here are some topics you could consider:

Of Mice and Men

1. What do you feel were Steinbeck's motives in writing this story? What was he trying to make us think about? Does it have any relevance for us today?
2. Was George right or wrong in taking a potentially dangerous person such as Lennie with him into work situations among persons who did not know him?
3. Discuss the social conditions under which the characters live and the effect these have on their lives.

The Pearl

4. Can this short novel be seen as a parable? If so, what is its message?
5. Might Kino have acted more prudently in trying to sell the pearl? Why did he go about things the way he did?
6. Do you think that Steinbeck was saying that Kino's race and class were happier when they did not try to better themselves, or do you think this is an inadequate response to the novel?

THE G.C.S.E. EXAMINATION

In this examination you many find that the set texts have been selected by your teacher from a very wide list of suggestions in the examination syllabus. The questions in the examination paper will therefore be applicable to many different books. Here are some questions you could answer by making use of these Steinbeck novels:

Of Mice and Men

1. Characters in stories are often led on by dreams of a wonderful future. From a book of your choice, explain what these are for one or more of the characters and discuss what has happened to these dreams by the end of the story.
2. Write about a novel in which loneliness is an important theme. Show its effect on one or more of the leading characters and the part it plays in the story.
3. Choose a book where close friendship is put to a severe test. Briefly outline the situation and then comment on how the friends emerge from this testing.

The Pearl

4. Explore the theme of human greed as it is presented in a book of your choice.
5. The lure of great treasure has been the theme of many books. Show how a character in a book you know responds to this, and comment on the effect it has on him or her and those around.
6. Write about a character in a book who has to struggle against those who are more rich and powerful then he or she is in order to obtain what is their due. Discuss the effect of the struggle on the character.

ESSAY QUESTIONS ON *OF MICE AND MEN* AND *THE PEARL*

Of Mice and Men

1. How far was Lennie the victim of other people's faults?
2. Describe the incident when Curley attacks Lennie in the bunkhouse. Explain how and why it began and make clear the reactions of Lennie, George and Slim.
3. Discuss George's feelings for Lennie. What do you think George gained from this difficult friendship?

The Pearl

4. What evidence is there that the society in which Kino lives makes it almost impossible for him to use the pearl to fulfil his dreams for himself and his family?
5. Describe and comment on the effect which the discovery of the pearl has on (a) Kino, (b) Juana and (c) the doctor.
6. How satisfying do you find the end of this story? Write about your feelings concerning Kino and Juana as the pearl is hurled into the sea.